Grades Pre K-2

Primary Level

IDEA BOOK

for Cuisenaire® Rods
Teacher's Resource Manual

Edited by: Karen Soll
Interior designed by: Robert Williams
Cover designed by: Dave Metzger

© 2002, 1977 Learning Resources, Inc.
® ETA/Cuisenaire®. Printed under license with ETA/Cuisenaire®, Vernon Hills, Illinois (U.S.A.)

Learning Resources, Inc. Vernon Hills, Illinois (U.S.A.)
Learning Resources Ltd., King's Lynn, Norfolk (U.K.)

All rights reserved. This book is copyrighted. No part of this book may be reproduced, stored in a retrieval system, or transmitted, in any form or by any means electronic, photocopying, recording, or otherwise, without written permission, except for the specific permission stated below.

Each blackline master is intended for reproduction in quantities sufficient for classroom use. Permission is granted to the purchaser to reproduce each blackline master in quantities suitable for noncommercial classroom use.

The word Cuisenaire® and the color sequence of the rods, cubes, and squares are registered trademarks of ETA/Cuisenaire®.

ISBN 1-56911-748-9

Printed in China.

TABLE OF CONTENTS

Topic	Page	Grades
Introduction	5	
Numbers and Operations		
Exploring the Rods	8	Pre K, K, 1, 2
Building and Storytelling with Rods	9	Pre K, K, 1, 2
Building Together	10	Pre K, K, 1, 2
Building Flat Designs	11	Pre K, K, 1, 2
Playing Follow the Leader	12	Pre K, K, 1, 2
Describing Relative Positions in Space	13	K, 1, 2
Developing Visual Memory	14	K, 1, 2
1-cm Graph Paper Master	15	Pre K, K, 1, 2
Recording with Play Dough	16	Pre K, K, 1, 2
Building a Staircase	17	Pre K, K, 1, 2
Building and "Photographing" Staircases	18	K, 1, 2
Playing the Staircase Game	19	K, 1, 2
Guessing the Rods	20	K, 1, 2
Listening to the Rods	21	K, 1, 2
Forming a Rhythm Band	22	Pre K, K
Marching with Rods	23	Pre K, K, 1, 2
Acting Out Rhymes	24	K, 1, 2
Building and Coloring on Graph Paper	25	Pre K, K, 1, 2
Sharing Designs	26	Pre K, K, 1, 2
Making Trains	27	Pre K, K, 1, 2
Finding Lengths of Trains	28	Pre K, K, 1, 2
Playing Challenge Match Game for Addends	29	1, 2
Playing Challenge Match Game for Many Addends	30	1, 2
Matching Longer Trains	31	K, 1, 2
Coding the Colors	32	K, 1, 2
Matching Rods with the Codes Game	33	K, 1, 2
Matching the Codes with Rods Game	34	K, 1, 2
Introducing the Plus Sign	35	K, 1, 2
Practicing the Plus Sign	36	K, 1, 2
Worksheet on Practicing the Plus Sign	37	K, 1, 2
Master for Work with Trains	38	K, 1, 2
Introducing the Equals Sign	39	K, 1, 2
Recording Rod Patterns	40	K, 1, 2
Completing Plus Stories	41	K, 1, 2
Worksheet on Completing Plus Stories 1	42	K, 1, 2
Worksheet on Completing Plus Stories 2	43	K, 1, 2
Coloring Rod Lengths	44	K, 1, 2
Worksheet on Coloring Rod Lengths 1	45	K, 1, 2
Worksheet on Coloring Rod Lengths 2	46	K, 1, 2
Matching Codes and Lengths	47	1, 2
Worksheet on Matching Codes and Lengths	48	1, 2
Singing about Rods and Numbers	49	K, 1, 2
Changing Rod Stories to Number Sentences	50	1, 2
Worksheet on Changing Rod Stories to Number Sentences	51	1, 2
Finding Sums	52	K, 1, 2
Worksheet on Finding Sums	53	K, 1, 2
Worksheet Master for Sums and Differences	54	K, 1, 2
Building an Addition Table	55	1, 2
Worksheet for Building an Addition Table	56	1, 2
Practicing Orange Plus Stories	57	1, 2
Finding Sums Greater Than 10	58	1, 2
Using Number Lines to Add	59	1, 2
Worksheet on Using Number Lines to Add	60	1, 2

TABLE OF CONTENTS

Topic	Page	Grades
Worksheet Master for Number Lines	61	1, 2
Making an Addition Table with Sums to 20	62	1, 2
Worksheet on Making an Addition Table	63	1, 2
Finding the Missing Rod	64	1, 2
Playing Challenge Match Game for Missing Addends	65	1, 2
Playing the I WISH I HAD Game	66	K, 1, 2
Playing Cuisenaire® Hopscotch	67	K, 1, 2
Solving the Case of the Missing Addend	68	1, 2
Practicing Missing Addends	69	1, 2
Subtracting by Finding How Much More	70	1, 2
Teaching Subtraction as Take Away	71	1, 2
Introducing the Minus Sign	72	1, 2
Writing Subtraction Stories	73	1, 2
Worksheet on Subtraction Stories 1	74	1, 2
Worksheet on Subtraction Stories 2	75	1, 2
Using Number Lines to Subtract	76	2
Worksheet for Number Line Subtraction	77	2
Relating Addition and Subtraction Stories	78	2
Hitting the Target Number	79	2
Playing the Trading Game for Addition	80	1, 2
Playing the Trading Game for Subtraction	81	2
Generating Multiples from One-Color Trains	82	1, 2
Finding Factors From One-Color Trains	83	2
Finding Halves	84	1, 2
Interpreting One-Color Trains as Fractional Parts	85	2

Topic	Page	Grades
Algebra		
Placing Rods in a Pattern	86	K, 1, 2
Making Rectangular Patterns	87	1, 2
Combining Two Staircases	88	K, 1, 2
Using the Commutative Property of Addition	89	1, 2
Exploring Even and Odd Numbers	90	1, 2
Exploring Patterns with Square Numbers	91	2
Playing Cuisenaire® Rod Mancala	92	1, 2
Master for Mancala Mat	93	1, 2
Playing Rod Mancala with Values	94	1, 2
Playing Mancala Going Round and Round	95	1, 2
Making Cuisenaire® Code Words	96	1, 2
Worksheet on Rod Code Words	97	1, 2
Worksheet Master for Rod Code Words	98	1, 2
Geometry		
Exploring Symmetry	99	K, 1, 2
Matching Designs Side-by-Side	100	K, 1, 2
Covering Designs in More Than One Way	101	K, 1, 2
Worksheet on Covering Designs in More than One Way 1	102	K, 1, 2
Worksheet on Covering Designs in More than One Way 2	103	K, 1, 2
Covering Designs with a Given Set of Rods	104	1, 2
Worksheet on Covering Designs 1	105	1, 2
Worksheet on Covering Designs 2	106	1, 2

TABLE OF CONTENTS

Topic	Page	Grades
Measurement		
Comparing Lengths of Rods	107	K, 1, 2
Using Rods to Measure Objects	108	K, 1, 2
Practicing Inequality Signs	109	1, 2
Playing the Comparing Game	110	1, 2
Finding Area of a Rod Design	111	1, 2
Worksheet on Area	112	1, 2
Finding Perimeter of a Rod Design	113	1, 2
Worksheet on Perimeter	114	1, 2
Data Analysis and Probability		
Conducting Surveys	115	K, 1, 2
Using Rods for Bar Graphs	116	K, 1, 2
Finding Rearrangements of Rods in a Train	117	1, 2
Finding All the Trains for a Given Rod	118	1, 2
Exploring Pascal's Triangle	119	2
Exploring Probability with Rod Codes	120	1, 2

INTRODUCTION

This revised and enhanced *Idea Book for Cuisenaire® Rods* at the primary level consists of 86 Learning Experiences, 22 Worksheets, and five Worksheet Masters. The book is divided into five sections related to the content standards for Pre K-2 published in 2000 by the National Council of Teachers of Mathematics (NCTM): Number and Operations, Algebra, Geometry, Measurement, Data Analysis and Probability. Even though these five sections have separate designations as indicated in the Table of Contents, there is a great deal of integration of topics. The five NCTM process standards (Problem Solving, Reasoning and Proof, Communication, Connections, and Representations) are fully embedded into the content standards, and are indicated at the bottom of each Learning Experience in the section entitled "Underlying Mathematics Related to NCTM Standards." The Underlying Mathematics lists have also been consolidated and summarized on pages 6 and 7 as an overview of both content and process.

Each Learning Experience is on a separate page and is presented in a consistent format for ease in use. The format includes a descriptive title, the appropriate grade level(s), the materials needed for the learning experience, suggested settings for classroom implementation, details about the learning experience for a description of each game or activity together with teaching suggestions and grade level adaptations, and the underlying mathematical concepts related to the learning experience. Cuisenaire Rods can be introduced at any of the grade levels, and many of the activities can be used fruitfully beyond Grade 2.

All of the Learning Experiences use Cuisenaire Rods, and many of them require 1-cm graph paper, for which a Master is provided on page 15. Cuisenaire Rods come in sets of 74 rods — 4 each of the orange, blue, brown, black, dark green, and yellow rods; 6 purple rods, 10 light green rods, 12 red rods, and 22 white rods. One set is generally sufficient for two to four children. Several activities use crayons matching the rod colors, and often blank paper and pencils are required. Other suggested materials are listed in the chart below along with the pages where they are needed.

Play dough for each child (Suggested recipe provided) (pg.16)	Bag (pg. 67)
An empty container for each pair or group of children (pg. 19, 20, 34, 110)	Scissors and transparent tape (pg. 68)
An empty can for each child (pg. 22, 66)	Extra white rods (pg. 80, 81, 82, 87, 91, 92, 115)
Index cards (pg. 32, 33, 34, 79, 120)	One die or two dice for each group (pg. 80, 81)
Crepe paper (optional) (pg. 66)	Mancala Mat (pg. 92, 93, 94, 95)
Colored construction paper (pg. 67, 68)	A mirror for each child (optional) (pg. 99)
Masking tape (pg. 67)	Meter stick (optional) (pg. 82, 108)

Note: When using Connecting Cuisenaire® Rods on graph paper or design worksheets, the connectors should fall outside the lines.

INTRODUCTION

The various settings are also listed in the chart below. Most of the activities that are designated as teacher-led can be pursued individually or in small groups once the ideas have been introduced. Children working as partners can free the teacher to aid other children, since the rods are very self-motivating and self-checking.

One child working individually	A small group led by the teacher
Two children working together	Ten or more children led by the teacher
Two children working individually	A whole class, children working individually
A small group, children working individually	A whole class, children working in pairs
A small group, children working in pairs	A whole class, children working in small groups
A small group, children working together	A whole class led by the teacher

Underlying Mathematics Related to NCTM Standards

Adding with many addends *(pg. 101-106, 111, 118, 119)*

Association of addends and sums *(pg. 28-31, 34, 39, 40-43, 49-52, 55-64, 80, 89, 101-106, 111, 112, 118-119)*

Association of codes with rods, lengths, or color names *(pg. 32-42, 47-48, 64, 79, 96)*

Association of colors with lengths *(pg. 17-20, 25, 26, 44-47)*

Association of colors with rods *(pg. 8-14, 23-26, 32-34, 86)*

Association of numbers with rods *(pg. 44-46, 52, 55, 73-78, 84-85)*

Association of 2-dimensional representations and 3-dimensional rods *(pg. 16, 25-26)*

Awareness of rod attributes (length, color, and shape) *(pg. 8-12, 16, 19-20, 25-26)*

Bodily-kinesthetic movements *(pg. 23-24, 67)*

Categorization *(pg. 115-116)*

Combinations (forming subsets of a given set) *(pg. 118-119)*

Comparisons of lengths *(pg. 19-20, 27, 107-110)*

Composite and prime numbers *(pg. 87)*

Communication and verbalization of findings *(pg. 19-22, 29-31, 35, 40, 55-56, 65-72, 80-81, 84-88, 90-100, 104-120)*

Communication and verbalization of ideas *(pg. 8-14, 16-18, 25, 27-28, 32-34, 64, 79, 101-103)*

Commutative property of addition *(pg. 89)*

Concepts of area and perimeter *(pg. 87, 111-114)*

Congruence of shapes *(pg. 12-14, 16, 99-100)*

Connections between addition, missing addends, and subtraction *(pg. 66-77, 110)*

Connections between arithmetic and geometry *(pg. 24, 30, 101-106, 108)*

Connections to art, music, or poetry *(pg.16, 21-24, 30)*

Connections to life experiences and other subjects *(pg. 8-11, 13, 100, 115-116)*

Counting *(pg. 9-10, 14, 27, 30, 33-34, 36-38, 44-48, 57-63, 87, 90-98, 108, 111-116)*

Dimensions of a square (length, width) *(pg. 91)*

Equality *(pg. 109-110)*

Equivalence of lengths *(pg. 108, 116)*

Even and odd numbers *(pg. 90-91)*

Expected outcomes *(pg. 120)*

Filling space with rods *(pg. 101-106, 109)*

Horizontal, vertical, and diagonal orientations *(pg. 11, 16, 25)*

Inequalities — less than, greater than, and between *(pg. 107-110)*

INTRODUCTION

Underlying Mathematics Related to NCTM Standards

Introduction to probability *(pg. 80-81, 120)*

Inverse relationship between addition and subtraction *(pg. 78-79)*

Letting rods other than white represent the value of one *(pg. 85)*

Logical thinking, reasoning, and strategic planning *(pg. 86, 88, 92-95)*

Meaning of addition *(pg. 27-28, 31, 35-43, 49-56, 68)*

Meaning of subtraction *(pg. 65-66, 70-77)*

Missing addends *(pg. 64-72)*

Money values *(pg. 101-103)*

Multiples of 2, 5, and 10 *(pg. 82, 94-98, 108)*

Multiplication as repeated addition *(pg. 82, 94-98, 101-103)*

One-to-one correspondence *(pg. 10, 12-14, 27, 110, 115-116)*

Ordering of lengths *(pg. 17-19, 21-24, 88, 107-108)*

Patterns, patterning, and functions *(pg. 86, 89, 91-95, 117-118)*

Permutations (arrangements of rod patterns) *(pg. 117-119)*

Powers of two *(pg. 119)*

Place value (tens and ones) *(pg. 57-63, 80, 81)*

Problem solving *(pg. 21-22, 88, 90-91, 94-98, 101-107, 111-112, 115-120)*

Readiness for multiplication and division *(pg. 82-83, 87, 94-96, 101-103, 108)*

Readiness for fractions *(pg. 84-85)*

Readiness for prime numbers *(pg. 83)*

Readiness for tens and ones *(pg. 31, 57-63, 80-81)*

Reasoning and proof *(pg. 17, 21-22, 28-31, 36-39, 44-48, 52-54, 65-77, 87-89, 94-98, 107-114, 117, 120)*

Recognition of equivalencies of lengths *(pg. 8-11, 12, 28-31, 35, 41-43, 49-54, 57-62, 65-78, 80-81, 89-90)*

Recognition of rod lengths *(pg. 17-19, 20, 23-24)*

Recognition of rod sounds *(pg. 21-22)*

Rectangular patterns *(pg. 87)*

Regrouping in addition and subtraction *(pg. 79-81)*

Representation of lengths in terms of white rods *(pg. 44-63, 80, 82, 90, 96-98, 101-106)*

Rod codes in people's names *(pg. 120)*

Seeing rods as relationships *(pg. 84-85, 90)*

Skip counting (pre-multiplication) *(pg. 90, 94-96, 108)*

Square numbers *(pg. 91)*

Symmetry *(pg. 11, 88, 99-100)*

Spatial vocabulary *(pg. 13)*

Use of addition sentences *(pg. 49-54, 78)*

Use of a table with rows and columns *(pg. 55-56, 62-63)*

Use of inequality symbols *(pg. 109)*

Use of subtraction sentences *(pg. 73-78)*

Use of the equal sign *(pg. 39-41, 49-54)*

Use of the minus sign *(pg.73-77)*

Use of the terms rod triple or triple of rods *(pg. 28)*

Use of the word plus and the plus sign *(pg. 27, 35-43)*

Visual thinking and visual memory of shapes *(pg. 12, 14, 17-20, 28-30, 32, 68-72, 99-100, 117)*

Grades: Pre K, K, 1, 2

EXPLORING THE RODS

Materials:
Cuisenaire® Rods for each child

Settings:
One child working individually
A small group, children working individually
A whole class, children working individually

Learning Experience:

Ask each child to take some rods and to explore with them. Let the children work on their own for some time. You will find that children start work immediately and that they are full of ideas. They will do a wide variety of things. Some children will sort by colors. Others will build flat designs. Some will build tall structures, and some will build objects related to their life experiences whether they be rural, urban, or suburban. Some will organize the rods by lengths in staircase patterns. Allow them to share with each other. The children will enjoy this.

When it seems appropriate, informally direct the children's exploration with questions, such as:

1. What are you making?
2. What do you notice about the rods?
3. How are the rods alike?
4. How are the rods different?
5. How many colors are there?
6. Can you name the colors?
7. How many lengths are there?
8. Does the same color always have the same length?
9. Does the same length always have the same color?

This activity should be repeated over several sessions so that each child has an opportunity to explore the rods in a variety of ways. Some children will also need more exploration time than others will.

Children also benefit from brief explorations at the beginning and end of more structured lessons with the rods. Free exploration allows children to pursue their own ideas and to make important discoveries. It is through informal exploration with rods that children develop intuitions for later mathematical work.

Underlying Mathematics Related to NCTM Standards:
Awareness of rod attributes (length, color, and shape)
Association of colors with rods
Recognition of equivalencies of lengths
Connections to life experiences
Communication and verbalization of ideas

Grades: Pre K, K, 1, 2

BUILDING AND STORYTELLING WITH RODS

Materials:
Cuisenaire® Rods for each child

Settings:
One child working individually
A small group, children working individually
A whole class, children working individually

Learning Experience:

Ask the children to build with their rods. Children often build in three dimensions rather than flat on the table. Encourage them to build creatively and to try balancing the rods on tall structures. Some creations will topple over, but that is a necessary part of the learning experience.

If possible, take some photos of the children's work. They'll enjoy seeing their own creations later in the year. These photographs or slides will also be excellent to display for parents.

When the children finish building, ask questions, such as:

1. How many of you used an orange rod in your design?
2. How many of you used all 10 colors?
3. How many of you built a flat design on the table?
4. How many of you built a tall structure?
5. What did you build? Describe it.
6. How many rods did you use in your design?

As an extension to having children build their own creations, ask each child to make the same design, such as a clown. Children may glance at each other's designs for ideas. After each child has built a clown, compare the various kinds of clowns and ask questions, such as:

1. Tell about your clown.
2. Does your clown have a hat?
3. Does your clown have big feet?
4. Does your clown have buttons? How many?
5. What colors did you use?
6. Does your clown have a name?
7. How many rods did you use for the mouth?
8. How many rods did you use in all?
9. What makes your clown special?
10. What shall we build next? (Perhaps a different kind of clown or a house, skyscraper, animal, truck, flower, or tree.)

Encourage children to tell and write stories about their structures. The storytelling aspect of rod work is very powerful.

Underlying Mathematics Related to NCTM Standards:
Awareness of rod attributes (length, color, and shape)
Association of colors with rods
Recognition of equivalencies of lengths
Counting
Connections to life experiences
Communication and verbalization of ideas

Grades: Pre K, K, 1, 2

BUILDING TOGETHER

Materials:
Cuisenaire® Rods for each child

Settings:
A small group, children working individually
A whole class, children working individually

Learning Experience:

Ask the children in each group to put all their rods in the center of the table. Each group builds a project as a team. The children develop a theme of their own creation. The two most challenging and creative aspects of this experience are for the children to carry out their theme using only the rods on the table and to think of uses for all of these rods. Some typical themes that children enjoy making are:

- a city
- a playground
- an amusement park
- a circus
- a ski resort
- our neighborhood
- a family
- the four seasons
- people who help us (policemen, nurses, firemen, etc.)
- a construction site
- a zoo with animals
- a farm
- a campground
- an airport
- various sports
- a spaceship
- characters from children's stories

The children enjoy telling stories and writing about their projects. They also love to tell about every aspect of their creations. This activity provides many opportunities for integration with other subject areas, such as reading, social studies, language arts, science, and art and can be repeated with different students working together each time. It is nice to photograph each project and the children involved. Both the stories and photographs can be shared with parents.

Have children put the rods back into individual sets as part of the learning experience. This can be done either by counting the number of each color rod required in a typical set or by sorting the rods by colors and putting them back in this manner. Both methods are useful mathematically; the first is based on counting and the second is based on one-to-one correspondence.

Underlying Mathematics Related to NCTM Standards:
Awareness of rod attributes (length, color, and shape)
Association of colors with rods
Recognition of equivalencies of lengths
Connections to life experiences
Communication and verbalization of ideas

Grades: Pre K, K, 1, 2

BUILDING FLAT DESIGNS

Materials:
Cuisenaire® Rods for each child
Blank paper for each child

Settings:
One child working individually
A small group, children working individually
A whole class, children working individually

Learning Experience:

Ask each child to build an object or design so that the rods remain flat on the table or floor. For this activity, rods may not be placed on top of each other to touch each other. Rods may be placed horizontally, vertically, or diagonally. For example:

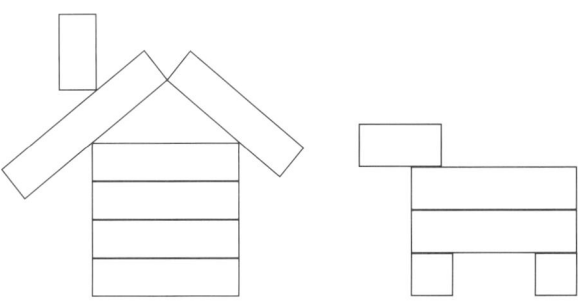 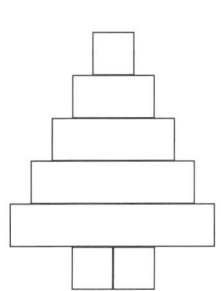 

Children may want to make pictures by putting the rods on a sheet of paper. The paper provides a workspace that some children need to define the task and sets the stage for them coloring rod pictures later on.

Some children will build a free-form design. Others will enjoy depicting something familiar such as a house, flower, dog, or pine tree.

In their free exploration with rods, children often create designs that are symmetrical like the flower and pine tree shown above. The portions of the design on both sides of a line of symmetry match. Children should be encouraged to recognize symmetrical designs and to think of examples of symmetry in life – nature, architecture, paintings, or interior decorations. This activity can help children be more aware of shape and form in their environment.

Underlying Mathematics Related to NCTM Standards:
Awareness of rod attributes (length, color, and shape)
Association of colors with rods
Recognition of equivalencies of lengths
Counting
Connections to life experiences
Communication and verbalization of ideas

Grades: Pre K, K, 1, 2

PLAYING FOLLOW THE LEADER

Materials:
Cuisenaire® Rods for each pair of children

Settings:
Two children working together
A small group, children working in pairs
A whole class, children working in pairs

Learning Experience:

The pairs of children should sit side-by-side. Ask one child in each pair to make a flat design using no more than 10 rods. After the first child completes the design, ask the second child to follow the leader by building an exact copy of the first child's design.

The partners check each other to be sure that the two designs are exactly alike and discuss why it was an easy or difficult design to match. Then, the children switch roles. The second child is the leader and makes the original design. The first child makes an exact copy. Again, they should discuss the challenge the design may have caused.

Children whose perceptual or motor skills are not well established may have difficulty with this experience. This activity is useful to help children develop perceptual ability, but should be postponed until they can achieve some degree of success.

An easier version of this activity is to play *Follow he Leader* one rod at a time. After the leader places each rod, the other child copies it. It may also be easier for some children to use fewer than six rods, though the designs will not be as interesting.

When the students become proficient with this activity, they can use more than 10 rods. The level of difficulty depends more on the perceptual ability of the children than on their age. As a further extension, the leader can add a few more rods to the original design after it has been copied, without the other child watching where the additional rods are placed. The additions will then need to be copied by the other child. Extending a design is often a challenge since the second child has to look at two designs at the same time and compare their differences.

Underlying Mathematics Related to NCTM Standards:
Awareness of rod attributes (length, color, and shape)
Association of colors with rods
Recognition of equivalencies of lengths
One-to-one correspondence
Congruence of shapes
Visual memory of shapes
Communication and verbalization of ideas

Grades: K, 1, 2

DESCRIBING RELATIVE POSITIONS IN SPACE

Materials:
Cuisenaire® Rods for each child
Blank paper for each child

Settings:
Two children working together
A small group, children working together in pairs
A whole class, children working in pairs

Learning Experience:

The rods lend themselves nicely to helping children understand the various words used to describe the relative position of two objects.

It is easiest if the children sit side-by-side rather than across from each other so that their spatial orientations are similar. Blank paper helps define a space for the children to place rods.

Left and Right:
Have the children place two rods on the paper and make statements like the following, filling in the correct colors: The _____ rod is to the left of the _____ rod. The _____ rod is to the right of the _____ rod.

Top and Bottom:
Ask the children to place a rod at the top of the page and have them say: The _____ rod is at the top of the page. Similarly, do the bottom of the page.

Other terms that should be experienced are <u>next to</u>, <u>beside</u>, <u>on top of</u>, <u>above</u>, <u>underneath</u>, <u>below</u>, <u>touching</u>, <u>not touching</u>, and the <u>horizontal</u>, <u>vertical</u>, and <u>diagonal</u> orientations.

When the children seem ready, they should test how well they can communicate. One child acts as the leader and selects six rods. The other child takes a collection of rods of the same six colors. A barricade of books is set between them. The first child makes a design and then proceeds to describe it to the other child who can't see it and has to make it just from the verbal description. The second child can ask questions for clarification. The children should be encouraged to use the vocabulary they just practiced.

When the children feel ready, the barricade of books is removed and the two designs are compared. The two designs should be identical. If they are not, the children discuss the differences and how they could have communicated more clearly. Then the children switch roles.

Underlying Mathematics Related to NCTM Standards:
Association of colors with rods
One-to-one correspondence
Congruence of shapes
Spatial vocabulary
Connections to life experiences and other subjects
Communication and verbalization of ideas

Grades: K, 1, 2

DEVELOPING VISUAL MEMORY

Materials:
1-cm Graph Paper for each child, page 15
Cuisenaire® Rods for each pair of children
Blank paper for each child

Settings:
Two children working together
A small group, children working in pairs
A whole class, children working in pairs

Learning Experience:

Ask one child in each pair to build a design on 1-cm graph paper using no more than six rods. The second child watches. When the design has been built, the second child studies it while the first child counts slowly to 10.

After 10 seconds have passed, the builder hides the rod design under a sheet of blank paper. The second child tries to build the same design from memory on the graph paper. Allow the children to take a second or third look if needed to help ensure success. They should also discuss the challenges that the design created.

Building on 1-cm graph paper rather than on plain paper helps the children orient the rods vertically, horizontally, and in a specific location on the sheet of paper.

This activity requires the children to deal abstractly with the specific length or color characteristics of the rods. It also calls upon the skill of visual memory. Visual memory or the lack of it has specific ramifications on success in many mathematical topics.

Building from memory may be too difficult an activity for some children. For those who are able to do it, it is a very empowering experience. Hence this type of activity should be repeated throughout the year so that children can experience improvement and success. Eventually many children will be able to copy a design from memory without needing successive looks.

More difficult versions of this experience would involve more than six rods, a picture of a colored rod design to be made from memory, and eventually uncolored rod designs to be made from memory. Free form designs on blank paper provide an even greater challenge.

Underlying Mathematics Related to NCTM Standards:
Association of colors with rods
Counting
One-to-one correspondence
Congruence of shapes
Visual memory of shapes
Communication and verbalization of ideas

1-CM GRAPH PAPER MASTER

Grades: Pre K, K, 1, 2

Grades: Pre K, K, 1, 2

RECORDING WITH PLAY DOUGH

Materials:
Cuisenaire® Rods for each child
Play dough for each child
(Suggested recipe below)

Settings:
One child working individually
A small group, children working in pairs

Learning Experience:

Give each child a piece of play dough. Either commercial or homemade play dough can be used. Ask children to help you make it as they certainly enjoy the preparation for this rod experience.

Help each child flatten a piece of play dough to about the thickness of one white rod and the size of half a sheet of paper. Each child then places rods on top of the play dough to make a design. The rods are pressed into the dough. When the rods are removed, the design remains. A hole may be made in the play dough to hang the plaque after the play dough hardens. The surface of the plaque may be painted to make it a colorful and attractive hanging.

Play Dough Recipe

2 cups all purpose flour (not self-rising)
1 cup salt
1 cup water
Food coloring (optional)

Combine flour and salt in a large flat-bottom bowl, and mix well. Add water a little at a time, mixing as you pour to form a ball. Additional water may be needed depending on humidity. Knead small amounts at a time for 9-10 minutes. Dough may be stored in a plastic bag in the refrigerator for up to 5 days. This recipe makes enough play dough for 4-5 children.

This experience could be part of an art lesson instead of being done during a mathematics class. Again, the notions of horizontal, vertical, and diagonal orientations of the rods can be discussed. If some rods have play dough remaining on them, they can be cleaned easily with a damp paper towel.

Underlying Mathematics Related to NCTM Standards:
Awareness of rod attributes (length, color, and shape)
Association of 2-dimensional representations with 3-dimensional rods
Horizontal, vertical, and diagonal orientations
Congruence of shapes
Connections to art
Communication and verbalization of ideas

BUILDING A STAIRCASE

Grades: Pre K, K, 1, 2

Materials:
1-cm Graph Paper for each child, page 15
Cuisenaire® Rods for each child

Settings:
A small group led by the teacher
A whole class led by the teacher

Learning Experience:

Ask each child to take one rod of each of the 10 colors and to build a staircase on 1-cm graph paper using the bottom horizontal line as a base line. The ten rods should be put in order according to their lengths, starting with the white rod and going in order from left to right all the way to the orange rod.

The children should note that the rods in the staircase increase each time by the length of a white rod. They should verify this fact by inserting and then removing a white rod successively for each jump of the stairs. This white rod should then be removed.

Ask the children to name the rods in order from smallest to largest while looking at and touching the rods in their staircase pattern:

> White, Red, Green, Purple,
> Yellow, Dark Green, Black,
> Brown, Blue, Orange

Naming the colors of the rods in order can be an exciting group experience when the teacher leads the group in unison. For fun, increase the speed each time the colors are said. If children do not know the color names, show each rod and name its color several times before building a staircase.

Some children may enjoy naming the sequence in another way, such as thinking of flavors to go along with the color of the rods (vanilla, strawberry, lime, grape, lemon, spearmint, licorice, chocolate, blueberry, orange). Encourage them to come up with ideas that help them remember the rod sequence.

The children may then wish to make another staircase going down from orange to white. Have them name the rods from orange to white going down the staircase. When children feel ready, they may wish to close their eyes while naming the colors. Keep in mind that mastery is not expected at this stage of development. Many more activities for learning the order of the rod colors follow.

Underlying Mathematics Related to NCTM Standards:
Association of colors with lengths
Ordering of lengths
Recognition of rod lengths
Visual memory of shapes
Reasoning and proof
Communication and verbalization of ideas

Grades: K, 1, 2

BUILDING AND "PHOTOGRAPHING" STAIRCASES

Materials:
Cuisenaire® Rods for each child
1-cm Graph Paper for each child, page 15
Crayons matching the rod colors for each child

Settings:
A small group led by the teacher
A whole class led by the teacher

Learning Experience:

Ask each child to build a staircase on the 1-cm Graph Paper with one rod of each color, using the bottom horizontal line as a base line. Direct the children to mark the top end of each rod and to color its length on the graph paper according to its correct rod color.

Once the staircases are colored, ask the children to sing the rod colors in unison with rhythm by two sets of five colors each.

**White, Red, Green, Pur-ple, Yel-low
Dark Green, Black, Brown, Blue, Or-ange**

A series of developmental steps might include:
Singing the five smallest rod colors:
- while looking at and touching the colored staircase picture
- while only looking at the colored staircase picture
- with eyes closed ("photographing" the staircase in their minds)
- in reverse order (yellow, purple, green, red, white)
- in forward and then reverse order

Singing the five largest colors:
- while looking at and touching the colored staircase picture
- while only looking at the colored staircase picture
- with eyes closed ("photographing" the staircase in their minds)
- in reverse order (orange, blue, brown, black, dark green)
- in forward and then reverse order

Singing all ten colors, using the suggested variations

Repeating this activity several times in succession helps children know the colors of the rods more automatically. Knowing the rods' colors well is important for later work with the rods.

Underlying Mathematics Related to NCTM Standards:
Association of colors with lengths
Ordering of lengths
Recognition of rod lengths
Visual memory of shapes
Communication and verbalization of ideas

PLAYING THE STAIRCASE GAME

Grades: K, 1, 2

Materials:
Cuisenaire® Rods for each pair of children
An empty container for each pair of children

Settings:
Two children working together
A small group, children working in pairs
A whole class, children working in pairs

Learning Experience:
The partners place two rods of each color in order into an empty container. As the rods are placed in the container, the children name the colors:

Two whites, two reds, two greens, two purples, two yellows

Two dark greens, two blacks, two browns, two blues, two oranges

Ask one child to shake the container so that the rods are thoroughly mixed. Taking turns, each child reaches into the container and takes out a rod without looking. The rods must be taken out in order from the smallest to largest, so the first rod that must be taken out is a white rod. As a correct rod is chosen, it is placed in a staircase pattern. If the rod chosen is not the next rod in the staircase, it must be put back into the container and the child waits for the next turn to select another rod. The first child to build a staircase in order from smallest to largest wins. Children will enjoy playing this game several times.

Vary the game by having both children build their staircases in order from largest to smallest. This time, the first rod that must be taken out is an orange rod. When children gain proficiency, they will feel comfortable having one child build from smallest to largest while the other builds from largest to smallest and then swapping roles.

While doing the activity, children should talk about which rods they mistake most frequently. The children's small hands can deal best with the five smallest rods and they'll also be able to find the orange rod with ease.

Underlying Mathematics Related to NCTM Standards:
Awareness of rod attributes (length, color, and shape)
Recognition of rod lengths
Ordering of lengths
Comparisons of lengths
Communication and verbalization of findings
Visual memory of shapes

Grades: K, 1, 2

GUESSING THE RODS

Materials:
Cuisenaire® Rods for each child
An empty container for each pair of children

Settings:
Two children working together
A small group, children working in pairs
A whole class, children working in pairs

Learning Experience:

Ask each child to make a staircase using one rod of each color. The partners place the 10 rods from one of the staircases in an empty container and shake it to mix them. The other staircase is left on the table for viewing.

One child names one of the 10 rods. The second child then tries to find that rod through touch by reaching inside the container without looking. The second child may look at the staircase on the table for help. Once the second child selects a rod, he or she takes it out and both children check to see that the named rod has been chosen. If not, the second child tries again. If the child does select the correct rod, it is put back into the container, and the children take turns naming and finding rods.

When the children feel confident, a more challenging game can be played. This time, one child in each pair closes his or her eyes and puts his or her hands behind his or her back. The second child selects a rod and places it in the first child's hands. The first child opens his or her eyes, looks at the staircase, and estimates which rod it is by touching and not looking at the rod. Three estimations are allowed. Then, the rod is put back into the container. The children take turns and keep score of correct guesses. The activity should be repeated for several rods.

This experience can be made easier by allowing the children to choose a known rod for them to hold. This rod serves as a frame of reference and can be chosen before or after the unknown rod is taken. Comparing the two rods by touching, but not looking, helps the child develop better tactile awareness.

If this game is too difficult for the children, start by using the five smallest rods: white, red, green, purple, and yellow. Then, use the five largest rods: dark green, black, brown, blue, and orange. When the children are ready, use all 10 rods.

Underlying Mathematics Related to NCTM Standards:
Awareness of rod attributes (length, color, and shape)
Recognition of rod lengths
Association of colors with length
Comparisons of lengths
Visual memory of shapes
Communication and verbalization of findings

LISTENING TO THE RODS

Grades: K, 1, 2

Materials:
Cuisenaire® Rods for each child
Cuisenaire® Rods for the teacher

Settings:
A small group led by the teacher
A whole group led by the teacher

Learning Experience:

Ask the children to be very quiet. Drop an orange rod onto a hard surface. Then drop a white rod onto the same surface. Ask the children to listen carefully as each rod is dropped. Ask the children to come up in turn to drop orange rods and then white rods and to describe what they notice about the sounds.

The children should notice that different rods make different sounds as the rods are dropped in order from white to orange. Drop the rods again in order from orange to white, and have the children drop individual rods again and name them.

Once the children are more familiar with the sounds, have them try the activity, but this time by closing their eyes. Then, drop a rod and ask the children if it was a big or a small rod. Drop the same rod again. The children will name some rods that it might be and some that it surely isn't. Have students identify a rod of which they know the sound and drop it. Then, drop the unknown rod again. The children will refine their guesses based on the new data.

Exact answers are not expected. This activity increases the children's awareness of sounds. Some useful questions that children enjoy exploring are:

1. Do the big rods make a louder noise than the smaller ones?
2. Does it matter whether you drop the rods from different heights?
3. Does it make a difference if you drop them gently or use some force?
4. Does the type of surface affect the sound?

Children can work in pairs to continue this activity provided the noise of one small group doesn't interfere with the other small groups. Some teachers use the corridor outside the classroom as expanded space. The children should be encouraged to formulate other questions and to discuss their findings.

Underlying Mathematics Related to NCTM Standards:
Ordering of lengths
Recognition of rod sounds
Connection to music
Problem solving
Reasoning and proof
Communication and verbalization of findings

Grades: Pre K, K

FORMING A RHYTHM BAND

Materials:
Cuisenaire® Rods for the teacher
An empty can for each child

Settings:
A small group led by the teacher
A whole class led by the teacher

Learning Experience:

Give each child a can and one rod to put in it. Tell the children to cover the containers with their hands and to shake them to make sounds. Make sure the cans do not have sharp edges.

Ask all the children with the same colored rod to shake their containers. Then, ask children with another color to shake their containers. Children will notice that rods of different colors make different sounds. They hopefully will have other questions. Discuss their questions, form hypotheses, and try to verify them. To promote classroom discussion, ask the following questions:

1. Does the size of the can make a difference?
2. Does the material of the can make a difference?
3. Does it matter how hard you shake the can?

Songs may be composed by listing colors of rods to be shaken in succession. For example:

Orange, red, white, yellow / yellow, green, blue, black

Red, dark green, orange, purple / brown, white, green, orange

Create correctly colored notes for the song, and post them for all to see. Then, point to each colored note and have the children with that color rod shake their containers. This activity is similar to the style of a bell choir, but with very different sounds.

If this activity seems too noisy for a classroom setting, it can be done outdoors at recess. The children enjoy being in these musical performances, and they like writing the rod colors to be used. Familiar songs can be accompanied by all the children shaking their containers while singing the words. Some easily adapted songs include *Old MacDonald Had a Farm*, *Hokey Pokey*, and *Jingle Bells*.

Underlying Mathematics Related to NCTM Standards:
Ordering of lengths
Recognition of rod sounds
Connections to music
Problem solving
Reasoning and proof
Communication and verbalization of findings

MARCHING WITH RODS

Grades: Pre K, K, 1, 2

Materials:
Cuisenaire® Rods for the teacher

Settings:
Ten or more children led by the teacher

Learning Experience:
Make a staircase and remind the children of the order of the rod colors. Then, give each child a rod so that all 10 colors are given. There will be repeats if there are more than 10 children. Lead the children in singing this adaptation of the song, *Oh When the Saints Come Marching In*. When a particular color is mentioned, the children holding the corresponding rod hold it as high as they can and march around. They keep marching as the other children successively join them. Repeat the verses as many times as you want the march to last.

Chorus: Oh when the rods come marching through,
Oh when the rods come marching through,
We can see all 10 colors,
When the rods come marching through.

Verse 1: Oh, there'll be white, and there'll be red
And there'll be green and purple, too.
We can see all those colors,
When the rods come marching through.

(Repeat Chorus.)

Verse 2: Then there'll be yellow, and dark green.
And there'll be black and brown and blue.
We can see all those colors,
When the rods come marching through.

(Repeat Chorus.)

Verse 3: The longest rod is yet to come.
We know that orange follows blue.
We can see all those colors,
When the rods come marching through.

(Repeat Chorus.)

Underlying Mathematics Related to NCTM Standards:
Association of colors with rods
Recognition of rod lengths
Ordering of lengths
Connections to music
Bodily-kinesthetic movements

© Learning Resources, Inc.

Idea Book for Cuisenaire® Rods at the Primary Level

Grades: K, 1, 2

ACTING OUT RHYMES

Materials:
Cuisenaire® Rods for each child

Settings:
A small group led by the teacher
A whole class led by the teacher

Learning Experience:

Ask each child to build two staircases, one from smallest to largest and one from largest to smallest. Lead the children in saying and acting out this rhyme. The poem should be written on the blackboard or on a chartboard so that the children can follow along with the words. Children can either stand or sit. They can look at their staircases for help in remembering the colors. Pause between verses for the children to be able to do the command.

Some of the children who like writing should be encouraged to write a poem that will help all the children learn the rod colors.

1. Cuisenaire colors in a row
   Up the staircase, we do go,
   White, red, green, and purple,

   Bob your head just like a turtle.
   (Pause for children to bob their heads.)

2. Yellow, dark green, black, and brown,
   Blue, and orange end the round.
   Clap your hands and touch the ground.
   (Pause for children to clap their hands and touch the ground.)

3. Cuisenaire colors in a row,
   Down the staircase, we do go,
   Orange, blue, brown, and black.
   Reach around and touch your back.
   (Pause for children to reach around to touch their back.)

4. Dark green, yellow, purple, and green
   Wash your face to make it clean. (Pause for children to pretend to wash their face.)

5. Red and white, no need to frown
   We know the staircase up and down. (Pause for children to reach high and then bend low.)

Underlying Mathematics Related to NCTM Standards:
Association of colors with rods
Recognition of rod lengths
Ordering of lengths
Connection to poetry
Bodily-kinesthetic movements

Grades: Pre K, K, 1, 2

BUILDING AND COLORING ON GRAPH PAPER

Materials:
1-cm Graph Paper for each child, page 15
Cuisenaire® Rods for each child
Crayons matching the rod colors for each child

Settings:
One child working individually
A small group, children working individually
A whole class, children working individually

Learning Experience:
Ask the children to build a flat design on 1-cm graph paper. In this activity, each rod must be placed horizontally or vertically (not diagonally) and must cover whole squares. Children may need to be shown the proper placement of the rods.

Horizontal

Vertical

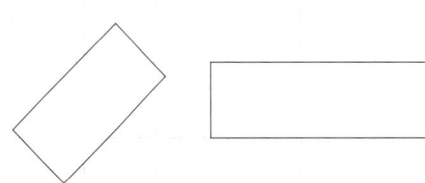
Not Allowed

Ask the children to color an exact picture of their designs. Demonstrate how to remove one rod at a time and how to color the squares that it covers with the appropriate Cuisenaire color. Then, ask the children to check their pictures by using the rods to rebuild the design.

Children will make a wide variety of designs. Be sure to have them share and discuss their designs. Generally, it is easier for young children to match rods to designs created by others than to color a rod picture. If this is a difficult activity, children can build designs on top of graph paper pictures made by others.

The activities in this experience help build readiness for future number work where the white rod is considered as being 1 unit. When appropriate, ask children how many squares in each case were colored: red (2), green (3), purple (4), yellow (5), dark green (6), black (7), brown (8), blue (9), and orange (10).

The designs made in this activity should be kept for later visual memory, addition, and area work.

Note: When using Connecting Cuisenaire® Rods on graph paper or design worksheets, the connectors should fall outside the lines.

Underlying Mathematics Related to NCTM Standards:
Association of colors with rods
Awareness of rod attributes (length, color, and shape)
Association of colors with lengths
Horizontal and vertical orientations
Association of 2-dimensional representations with 3-dimensional rods
Association of 3-dimensional rods with 2-dimensional representations
Communication and verbalization of ideas

Grades: Pre K, K, 1, 2

SHARING DESIGNS

Materials:
1-cm Graph Paper for each child, page 15
Cuisenaire® Rods for each child
Crayons matching the rod colors for each child

Settings:
A small group led by the teacher
A whole class led by the teacher

Learning Experience:

Ask each child to make a design with rods on the graph paper. Remind the children that each rod must be placed so that it is horizontal or vertical and covers whole squares. Then have the children outline each rod in their design and color it according to the correct Cuisenaire color.

Once the graph paper designs are colored, have children exchange their designs with one another. Each child then builds the new design by placing rods on top of the picture. Check each child's rod design for accuracy. You'll notice that some children will have difficulty matching the design exactly and may overlap edges.

Some children in grades 1 and 2 may be ready to reproduce a pictured design with rods placed on a separate sheet of graph paper rather than building on top of a colored design. Many Pre Kindergarten and Kindergarten children can build on top of a simple pictured design, whereas it might be difficult for them to outline and color on the graph paper. Going from the two-dimensional picture to the three-dimensional rods is easier than going from the three-dimensional rods to the two-dimensional representation. An even more abstract process would be to build a rod design from an uncolored picture where only the outlines of the rods are given.

Some rod discoveries that the children make include:

1. Only one length is associated with each color.
2. Only one color is associated with each length.
3. The color can be determined by counting the number of squares on the 1-cm graph paper.

white	1	dark green	6
red	2	black	7
green	3	brown	8
purple	4	blue	9
yellow	5	orange	10

Underlying Mathematics Related to NCTM Standards:
Association of colors with rods
Awareness of rod attributes (length, color, and shape)
Association of colors with lengths
Association of 2-dimensional representations with 3-dimensional rods
Association of 3-dimensional rods with 2-dimensional representations

MAKING TRAINS

Grades: Pre K, K, 1, 2

Materials:
Cuisenaire® Rods for each child
Cuisenaire® Rods for the teacher

Settings:
A small group led by the teacher
A whole class led by the teacher

Learning Experience:

Demonstrate a train by placing two rods end-to-end. For example, show a green rod and a yellow rod end-to-end. Describe this train in two ways:

G	Y

1. This is a train with two rods.
2. This is a train showing green plus yellow.

Then, show a train that has a red, white, and purple rod in that order left to right. Describe this train in two ways:

1. This is a train with three rods.
2. This is a train showing red plus white plus purple.

Ask the children to make trains by placing rods end-to-end that fulfill certain conditions, such as:

1. A train with three cars all the same color.
2. A four-car train with a black engine and red caboose.
3. A short train that has lots of cars.
4. A long train that has only a few cars.
5. A train with four cars all the same color.
6. A five-car train with a dark green engine and green caboose.
7. A one-car train.

The children should describe their trains by naming the colors they used left to right using the word "plus" between the color names. Trains are very important since they provide a model for addition.

This exercise should be kept light and fun. It helps children process verbal commands. It also develops creativity, as children are able to respond to each command with many right answers. It helps them verbalize a visual situation as they name the colors and gives them confidence as they make commands for other children to follow.

Underlying Mathematics Related to NCTM Standards:
Meaning of addition
Use of the word plus
Comparisons of lengths
Counting
One-to-one correspondence
Communication and verbalization of ideas

Grades: Pre K, K, 1, 2

FINDING LENGTHS OF TRAINS

Materials:
Cuisenaire® Rods for each child
Cuisenaire® Rods for the teacher

Settings:
A small group led by the teacher
A whole class led by the teacher

Learning Experience:

Ask the children to place a yellow rod and a red rod end-to-end. Then ask the children to find a one-car train that matches this two-car train. Some children may try several rods beside the two-car train before they find the black rod that matches exactly. The results can be stated in an addition sentence: yellow plus red equals black. The cars in the two-car train are called <u>addends</u>, and the one-car train that matches is called the sum.

Also when a third rod matches a two-car train, this configuration is called a <u>rod triple</u> or a <u>triple of rods</u>. Ask the children to build several rod triples like this. Have the children choose the two-car trains from the five smallest rods so that the result is always a one-car train. For example:

1. white plus red equals green.
2. green plus green equals dark green.
3. yellow plus green equals brown.
4. purple plus green equals black.

Students will enjoy creating problems for the class to solve and verifying the results. Once they've worked with the smallest rods, consider giving them other examples where longer rods are used, but results will still be a one-car train. For example:

1. dark green plus white equals black.
2. dark green plus red equals brown.
3. black plus green equals orange.
4. blue plus white equals orange.

If the students try something like black plus yellow, simply say that the sum is longer than an orange rod, or that it is more than orange. Please note that "Orange plus" stories for sums greater than orange are developed on pages 31 and 57. Sums greater than 10 are developed on page 58.

Underlying Mathematics Related to NCTM Standards:
Recognition of equivalencies of lengths
Use of the terms rod triple or triple of rods
Meaning of addition
Use of the terms addend and sum
Association of sums with addends
Visual thinking
Communication and verbalization of ideas
Reasoning and proof

Grades: 1, 2

PLAYING CHALLENGE MATCH GAME FOR ADDENDS

Materials:
Cuisenaire® Rods for each pair of children

Settings:
Two children working together
A small group, children working in pairs
A whole class, children working in pairs

Learning Experience:

Once students are used to matching two-car trains with the rod that gives the sum of the two addends, they enjoy doing the reverse process. Given any rod (other than white), they should be able to find a two-car train that will match. For example, if the challenge is a yellow rod, it is possible to make the following two-car trains:

1. white plus purple
2. red plus green
3. green plus red
4. purple plus white

Rules for Challenge Match Game for Addends:
Place about 40-50 assorted rods in the center of the table for each pair of children. The first player chooses a rod (other than white) and challenges the second player to make a two-car train that matches it. The second player states the plus sentence and keeps the triple of rods once the match has been made. Depending on the visual skills of the players, they may need to try various rods before attaining a match.

Then, the second player chooses a rod and challenges the first player to make a two-car train that matches it. The white rod can never be used as the challenge. The first player states the plus sentence and keeps the triple of rods once the match has been made.

The players reverse roles again. The pile of rods in the center of the table gets smaller each time. The object of the game is to "stump your partner" by choosing a single rod for which no two-car train can be made from the rods left in the center of the table.

The player who makes the challenge that cannot be matched is the winner of the game and scores one point for each rod left in the center of the table. Score may be accumulated from game to game. Children should play this game several times, since it helps them build readiness for work with addends.

Underlying Mathematics Related to NCTM Standards:
Recognition of equivalencies of lengths
Association of two addends for a sum
Visual thinking
Communication and verbalization of findings
Reasoning and proof

Grades: 1, 2

PLAYING CHALLENGE MATCH GAME FOR MANY ADDENDS

Materials:
Cuisenaire® Rods for each child
An empty container for each pair of children

Settings:
Two children working together
A small group, children working in pairs
A whole class, children working in pairs

Learning Experience:

This game follows the rules for the *Challenge Match Game for Addends* on page 29, but children are allowed to make a train with any number of rods, not just two-car trains. Since one-car trains are allowed, the white rod can be used as a challenge. In fact, every rod can be matched with a one-car train of the same color. About 40-50 assorted rods should be placed in the center of the table for each pair of children.

Rules for Challenge Match Game for Many Addends:
The first player chooses a rod and places it in front of the second player as a challenge. The second player must match the given rod with a train that can contain any number of cars. Even a one-car train equivalent to the given rod is allowed. The second player states the plus sentence and keeps all the rods involved in the match.

The players reverse roles. The second player challenges the first player to match a rod with a train. The players reverse roles again and again. The pile of rods in the center of the table gets smaller each time. The player who is first to pose a challenge in which the other player cannot make a train wins. The winner scores one point for each rod left in the center of the table.

As a variation, partners take on a challenge together rather than challenging each other. The goal is to use each rod in the pile so that it is matched with a train. One-car trains are allowed, and as the game comes to a close, children can shift rods around and use already-used rods in order to try to complete the task.

At the end of the activity, all rods should be matched with a train. With good thinking and planning, this task can almost always be done to completion starting with any random collection of 40-50 rods.

Underlying Mathematics Related to NCTM Standards:
Recognition of equivalencies of lengths
Association of two addends for a sum
Visual thinking
Counting
Communication and verbalization of findings
Reasoning and proof

Grades: K,1,2

MATCHING LONGER TRAINS

Materials:
Cuisenaire® Rods for each child

Settings:
A small group led by the teacher
A whole class led by the teacher

Learning Experience:

Ask the children to place a yellow rod and a blue rod end-to-end. Explain that there is no one-car train that matches this two-car train.

Ask the children to find a two-car train that will match the train yellow plus blue. There are many correct answers:

1. blue plus yellow
2. black plus black
3. brown plus dark green
4. dark green plus brown
5. purple plus orange
6. orange plus purple

Explain that when a two-car train is longer than orange, it is customary to match its length with "Orange plus . . ." This exercise builds readiness for sums greater than 10 being expressed by "10 plus . . ."

Ask the children to find the "orange plus" two-car trains that match each of these trains:

1. red plus blue (answer: orange plus white)
2. black plus yellow (answer: orange plus red)
3. brown plus purple (answer: orange plus red)
4. yellow plus dark green (answer: orange plus white)
5. brown plus black (answer: orange plus yellow)
6. blue plus blue (answer: orange plus brown)

Now ask the children to make questions about any two-car trains for the class to find either the one-car train or the orange plus train that will match. Children always enjoy playing the role of the teacher asking the questions of their classmates.

Y	E
O	P

Underlying Mathematics Related to NCTM Standards:
Recognition of equivalencies of lengths
Meaning of addition
Association of sums with addends
Readiness for tens and ones
Reasoning and proof
Communication and verbalization of findings

W	for	White
R	for	Red
G	for	Green
P	for	Purple
Y	for	Yellow
D	for	Dark Green
K	for	blacK
N	for	browN
E	for	bluE
O	for	Orange

Grades: K, 1, 2

CODING THE COLORS

Materials:
Cuisenaire® Rods for each child
Ten index cards for the teacher

Settings:
A small group led by the teacher
A whole class led by the teacher

Learning Experience:

Explain the definition of the term "nickname" to the children. Use examples from the children in the class. Then discuss the need for a quick way to name each rod. Since one major characteristic of the rods is color, the color names are used to devise a code for the rods. The convention is to use a single letter to stand for the color name of each rod. For the first six rods, the first letters of the color names are used:

W	for	White
R	for	Red
G	for	Green
P	for	Purple
Y	for	Yellow
D	for	Dark Green

Since black, brown, and blue all begin with the same first letter, their last letters are used for the code.

K	for	blacK
N	for	browN
E	for	bluE

Notice that the O for Orange should be written in a way that distinguishes it from the symbol for zero. Often a script O with a tail is used. Either capital letters or small letters can be used for rod codes. Since most young children are more familiar with recognizing and writing capital letters, they are used throughout the activities in this book.

Make a deck of cards with the code letters on them.

Choose a card at random and hold it up. Have the children hold the appropriate rod over their heads and say the correct color name for the code letter. If you face the class, it is easy to see which children do not choose the correct rods immediately. Let the children self-correct with as many tries as needed to be successful. Do this activity several times, speeding up the pace with which the students must make the association between rod color and code.

Underlying Mathematics Related to NCTM Standards:
Association of colors with rods
Association of codes with rods
Association of rods with codes
Visual memory
Communication and verbalization of ideas

Grades: K, 1, 2

MATCHING RODS WITH THE CODES GAME

Materials:
Cuisenaire® Rods for each group
Thirty index cards for each group

Settings:
A small group, children working together
A whole class, children working in small groups

Learning Experience:

Make a deck of 30 cards for each group, consisting of three cards for each of the 10 rod codes,
W, R, G, P, Y, D, K, N, E, O.

One player in each group acts as dealer and does not play. The dealer shuffles the deck of 30 code cards and places it facedown in the center of the table. Then he or she gives each player one rod of each of the ten colors.

On each round, the dealer turns one card faceup. The first player to put the correct rod on top of this code card wins the card and recovers the rod to use in future trials. The game ends when the deck of cards runs out. The player who has accumulated the most cards wins. Children may wish to score one point for each card they have won and accumulate scores for several games. Promote classroom discussion with the following questions after gameplay:

1. Did anyone get the same three codes during gameplay?
2. Did anyone get the same two codes during gameplay?
3. Who got a W card?
4. Who got an R card?
5. Who got a G card? (Ask the same question all the way to an O card.)
6. Did the sum of all of the players' scores for each game add to 30?

Have the children put their cards in order to see if they are missing any of the codes. Make sure that any missing codes get associated with the correct rod color in the children's minds by having them practice matching the rod color to the code.

This game is enjoyable for children to play during free time and need not be played during scheduled mathematics time.

Underlying Mathematics Related to NCTM Standards:
Association of colors with rods
Association of codes with rods
Association of rods with codes
Counting
Communication and verbalization of ideas

W	for	White
R	for	Red
G	for	Green
P	for	Purple
Y	for	Yellow
D	for	Dark Green
K	for	blacK
N	for	browN
E	for	bluE
O	for	Orange

Grades: K, 1, 2

MATCHING THE CODES WITH RODS GAME

Materials:
Cuisenaire® Rods for each group
Thirty index cards for each group
An empty container for each group

Settings:
A small group, children working together
A whole class, children working in small groups

Learning Experience:

Make a deck of 30 cards for each group, consisting of three cards for each of the 10 rod codes,
W, R, G, P, Y, D, K, N, E, O.

One player in each group acts as dealer and does not play. The dealer shuffles the deck of 30 code cards and deals five cards to each person. Each player holds the cards so that the others cannot see. The dealer stacks the remaining cards facedown on the table.

The rods are placed in an empty container. The dealer says "Go" and takes a rod from the container. The first player to put the correct code card faceup in the center of the table wins the card. The rod is put back in the container. The winning player draws another card from the playing deck in the center of the table so as to maintain five cards in hand. Gameplay ends when all the cards from the playing deck have been used. The player who has collected the most cards wins. The remaining cards in the players' hands are not counted as score.

After gameplay, promote classroom discussion with the following questions:

1. Did anyone get the same three codes during gameplay?
2. Did anyone get the same two codes during gameplay?
3. Who has a W card?
4. Who has an R card? (Ask the same question all the way to an O card.)
5. What codes didn't you get?
6. What rods are associated with these codes?

This game is enjoyable for children to play during free time and need not be played during scheduled mathematics time. Alternate between this game and *Matching Rods with the Codes Game* on page 33 to reinforce the connections between rods and the color codes for their color names.

Underlying Mathematics Related to NCTM Standards:
Association of colors with rods
Association of codes with rods
Association of rods with codes
Counting
Communication and verbalization of ideas

W	for	White
R	for	Red
G	for	Green
P	for	Purple
Y	for	Yellow
D	for	Dark Green
K	for	blacK
N	for	browN
E	for	bluE
O	for	Orange

Grades: K, 1, 2

INTRODUCING THE PLUS SIGN

Materials:
Cuisenaire® Rods for each child

Settings:
A small group led by the teacher
A whole class led by the teacher

Learning Experience:

Ask the children to make all the two-car trains for the purple rod and to describe each train in words.

P		
W	G	purple
R	R	white plus green
G	W	red plus red
		green plus white

(table layout: P spans top; W+G; R+R; G+W)

- P — purple
- W G — white plus green
- R R — red plus red
- G W — green plus white

Now introduce the symbol "+" for "plus," and record each two-car train with coding:

    W + G   R + R   G + W

Ask the children to make all the two-car trains for the yellow rod and record each train with coding (W + P, R + G, G + R, P + W). Then, write these plus stories on the board and have the children build the trains:

    R + D   G + Y   D + G
    E + W   P + Y   K + R
    N + R   W + Y   R + K

The children should say the colors that correspond to the codes. The use of coding doesn't need to be viewed as algebraic. The letter should be read as a color name and not as an alphabet name. For example, D + P is read as "dark green plus purple." The purpose of the coding is to provide a shorthand way to share the information in writing. At this stage, children do not need to match each train with a single rod to find the sum. The purpose of this activity is to just introduce the plus sign.

Underlying Mathematics Related to NCTM Standards:
- Recognition of equivalencies of lengths
- Association of codes with rods
- Association of rods with codes
- Association of codes with color names
- Meaning of addition
- Use of the plus sign
- Communication and verbalization of findings

W	for	White
R	for	Red
G	for	Green
P	for	Purple
Y	for	Yellow
D	for	Dark Green
K	for	blacK
N	for	browN
E	for	bluE
O	for	Orange

Grades: K, 1, 2

PRACTICING THE PLUS SIGN

Materials:
Worksheet on Practicing the Plus Sign, page 37
Master for Work with Trains, page 38
Cuisenaire® Rods for each child
Crayons matching the rod colors for each child
Pencil for each child

Settings:
One child working individually
A small group, children working individually
A whole class, children working individually

Learning Experience:

To reinforce the use of the plus sign, children need to be given plus stories and to build and then color the corresponding train. This work can be carried out on the Worksheet for Practicing the Plus Sign on page 37. You can also provide similar problems, and then have the children use the Master for Work with Trains on page 38 to fill in the answer. This page can also be used for children to write the plus stories for previously colored trains.

Using the worksheet, children should look at the letter codes, say the color names, get the rods, place them end-to-end on the strip, and then color the lengths with the appropriate colors. Since the strips are gridded by the length of a white rod, children can color the length of each rod by counting the number of white rods equivalent to the rod rather than estimating by eye. The activities show pictorially the relationship of each rod to the number of white rods that match it. The number of colored squares equals the number of white rods that matches. These worksheets precede the more abstract stage of using numerals. At this stage, children are not expected to match each train with a single rod to find the sum. The purpose of this activity is just to practice the plus sign.

These worksheets are self-checking by the children. Children can verify their work by looking at the color and finding the corresponding rod to place on the strip. The rod should match the colored length. Having the children check their work on a second day means that each worksheet can provide two worthwhile experiences.

Underlying Mathematics Related to NCTM Standards:
Association of codes with color names
Association of codes with rods
Association of rods with codes
Counting
Meaning of addition
Use of the plus sign
Reasoning and proof

W	for	White
R	for	Red
G	for	Green
P	for	Purple
Y	for	Yellow
D	for	Dark Green
K	for	blacK
N	for	browN
E	for	bluE
O	for	Orange

WORKSHEET ON PRACTICING THE PLUS SIGN

Grades: K,1,2

Name: Date:

Color the train picture for each plus story.

W	for	White	D	for	Dark Green
R	for	Red	K	for	blacK
G	for	Green	N	for	browN
P	for	Purple	E	for	bluE
Y	for	Yellow	O	for	Orange

① P + Y

② D + R

③ G + K

④ K + E

⑤ N + D

⑥ Y + D

© Learning Resources, Inc.   Idea Book for Cuisenaire® Rods at the Primary Level

Grades: K, 1, 2

MASTER FOR WORK WITH TRAINS

Name: _____ Date: _____

❶

❷

❸

❹

❺

❻

❼

❽

Grades: K, 1, 2

INTRODUCING THE EQUALS SIGN

Materials:
Cuisenaire® Rods for each child
Cuisenaire® Rods for the teacher
Paper and pencil for each child

Settings:
A small group led by the teacher
A whole class led by the teacher

Learning Experience:

Ask the children to build a two-car train with red plus black and to find the single rod that matches it.

Now introduce the symbol "=" for "is equal to," or "equals."

R + K = E is read as "red plus black equals blue."

Hold up a train made with the two rods. Ask the children to find the single rod that matches the rod pair and then to write the plus story using the rod codes, the plus sign, the equal sign, and the sum. Here are just a few examples:

green plus white	G + W = P
purple plus yellow	P + Y = E
red plus brown	R + N = O
black plus red	K + R = E
yellow plus yellow	Y + Y = O

dark green plus green	D + G = E
yellow plus red	Y + R = K
purple plus red	P + R = D
brown plus white	N + W = E
black plus red	K + R = E

The purpose of this activity is to introduce the equal sign so that a complete plus story can be written. At this stage of development, select examples that don't exceed orange. Lengths beyond orange will be further developed on pages 57 and 58. Children should verify their answer by showing the rod triples.

Underlying Mathematics Related to NCTM Standards:
Association of codes with rods
Association of addends with sums
Use of the plus sign
Use of the equal sign
Meaning of addition
Reasoning and proof

© Learning Resources, Inc.

Idea Book for Cuisenaire® Rods at the Primary Level

Grades: K, 1, 2

RECORDING ROD PATTERNS

Materials:
Cuisenaire® Rods for each child
Paper and pencil for each child

Settings:
Two children working together
A small group, children working in pairs
A whole class, children working in pairs

Learning Experience:

Ask the children to work together to build all the two-car trains that match a dark green rod. One child should then record the rod patterns using codes, while the other child reads the rod story.

Codes	Words
D = W + Y	"Dark green equals white plus yellow."
D = R + P	"Dark green equals red plus purple."
D = G + G	"Dark green equals green plus green."
D = P + R	"Dark green equals purple plus red."
D = Y + W	"Dark green equals yellow plus white."

The partners should build all the two-car trains for the other rods, with one child recording the rod patterns using codes and the other reading the rod story using color words. For example, the two-car trains for the black rod are:

K = W + D	K = D + W
K = R + Y	K = Y + R
K = G + P	K = P + G

Encourage children to discuss the patterns they observe. Some may notice that as one addend increases the other addend decreases, as shown with the example for the dark green rod. They may also observe that the order of the two cars in a train can be reversed, as shown in the example above for the black rod. The reversing of the addends to produce the same sum is an important property, known as the commutative property of addition. This is presented more formally on page 89.

Underlying Mathematics Related to NCTM Standards:
Association of addends with sums
Association of codes with rods
Use of the plus sign
Use of the equal sign
Meaning of addition
Communication and verbalization of findings

W	for	White
R	for	Red
G	for	Green
P	for	Purple
Y	for	Yellow
D	for	Dark Green
K	for	blacK
N	for	browN
E	for	bluE
O	for	Orange

COMPLETING PLUS STORIES

Grades: K, 1, 2

Materials:
Worksheet on Completing Plus Stories 1, page 42
Worksheet on Completing Plus Stories 2, page 43
Master for Work with Trains, page 38
Cuisenaire® Rods for each child
Crayons matching the rod colors for each child
Pencil for each child

Settings:
One child working individually
A small group, children working individually
A whole class, children working individually

Learning Experience:

The worksheets on pages 42 and 43 provide children with the opportunity to find the rod triple from plus stories that are given in codes. Then they color it on the gridded strips and write the entire plus story. You may need to reiterate the procedure and the meaning of the symbols.

Have children start by finding the rods indicated by the codes to make the two-car train. From there, the children can find the sum, or single rod length, and record the plus story. The meaning of "+" is reinforced as "making a train." The equal sign indicates the equivalence in length between the two-car train and the single rod that matches.

The addition process is done at the concrete level of finding the single car length that matches the train. The recording process is done on a pictorial level when the children color the plus stories and on an abstract level when they write the plus stories in codes.

The intermediate step of coloring the single car length may become the final step if the children are not ready to deal with abstract symbols. They will be able to say the colors in the plus stories rather than write the plus stories. The coloring of the rods on 1-cm graph paper is the precursor to establishing number values for the rods in terms of white rods.

Worksheet Answer Keys

Completing Plus Stories 1, page 42

1. W + K = N	4. P + P = N
2. G + Y = N	5. R + W = G
3. N + R = O	

Completing Plus Stories 2, page 43

1. Y + G = N	4. W + E = O
2. D + W = K	5. G + P = K
3. R + N = O	

You can create more examples using the Master for Work with Trains on page 38. In matching the rods to the 1-cm graph paper strips, children are building readiness for numerical sums. The plus stories with the rods can lead into interesting addition sentences with numbers, with the white rod being assigned the numerical value of 1.

Underlying Mathematics Related to NCTM Standards:
Association of codes with rods
Recognition of equivalencies of lengths
Association of addends with sums
Meaning of addition
Use of the plus sign
Use of the equal sign

W	for	White	D	for	Dark Green
R	for	Red	K	for	blacK
G	for	Green	N	for	browN
P	for	Purple	E	for	bluE
Y	for	Yellow	O	for	Orange

Grades: K, 1, 2

WORKSHEET ON COMPLETING PLUS STORIES 1

Name: Date:

Color the train picture for each plus story. Find and color the rod that matches each train. Use codes to write the complete plus story.

1) W + K

_____

2) G + Y

_____

3) N + R

_____

4) P + P

_____

5) R + W

_____

W	for	White	D	for	Dark Green
R	for	Red	K	for	blacK
G	for	Green	N	for	browN
P	for	Purple	E	for	bluE
Y	for	Yellow	O	for	Orange

42   Idea Book for Cuisenaire® Rods at the Primary Level   © Learning Resources, Inc.

WORKSHEET ON COMPLETING PLUS STORIES 2

Grades: K, 1, 2

Name: _____ Date: _____

Color the train picture for each plus story. Find and color the rod that matches each train. Use codes to write the complete plus story.

❶ Y + G

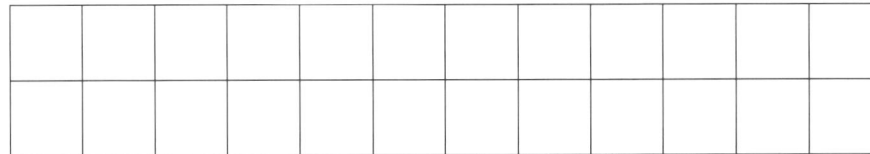

_____

❷ D + W

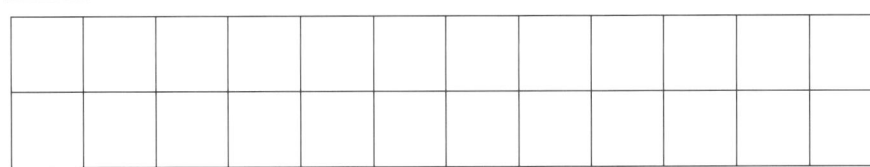

_____

❸ R + N

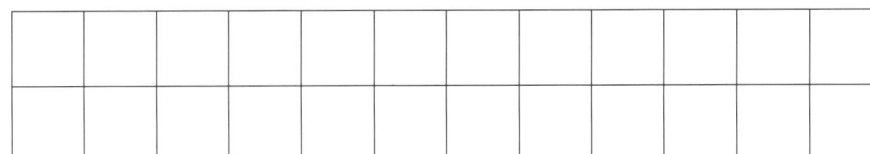

_____

❹ W + E

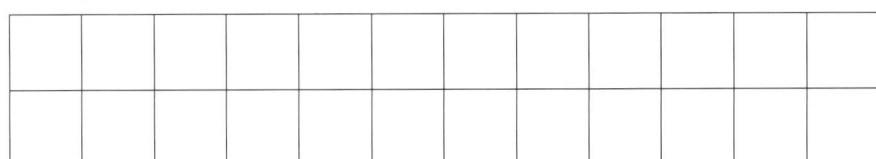

_____

❺ G + P

_____

W	for	White	D	for	Dark Green
R	for	Red	K	for	blacK
G	for	Green	N	for	browN
P	for	Purple	E	for	bluE
Y	for	Yellow	O	for	Orange

© Learning Resources, Inc. Idea Book for Cuisenaire® Rods at the Primary Level

Grades: K, 1, 2

COLORING ROD LENGTHS

Materials:
Worksheet on Coloring Rod Lengths 1, page 45
Worksheet on Coloring Rod Lengths 2, page 46
Cuisenaire® Rods for each child
Crayons matching the rod colors for each child

Settings:
One child working individually
A small group, children working individually
A whole class, children working individually

Learning Experience:

In order for children to change rod stories into number sentences, they need to know the equivalence of each rod, or the number of white rods required to match each rod. The Worksheets on pages 45 and 46 help children translate sets of white rods to single rods. They encourage the transfer from the concept of number as a set of discrete objects to the concept of number as a continuous length.

For example, 6 white rods can be thought of as 6 ones, while the dark green rod can be thought of as 1 six. Both approaches to number are important. The discrete model appeals to more analytical processing, and the continuous model encourages perceptual approaches.

In completing these sheets, some children will put the given number of white rods end-to-end in a train and then find the rod that matches the train. Others will count the number of white rods represented on the strip and match a rod to the length on the strip. The children may find it helpful to have a staircase of rods in front of them as they do these worksheets. The coloring stage reinforces the relationship of each rod color to its equivalent number of white rods.

Worksheet Answer Keys

Coloring Rod Lengths 1, page 45

1. 9W = E	6. 8W = N
2. 2W = R	7. 4W = P
3. 5W = Y	8. 7W = K
4. 10W = O	9. 6W = D
5. 3W = G	

Coloring Rod Lengths 2, page 46

1. 8W = N	6. 10W = O
2. 3W = G	7. 2W = R
3. 5W = Y	8. 9W = E
4. 7W = K	9. 1W = W
5. 6W = D	

Underlying Mathematics Related to NCTM Standards:
Representation of lengths in terms of white rods
Association of colors with lengths
Counting from 1 to 10
Association of numbers with rods
Reasoning and proof

W	for	White	D	for	Dark Green
R	for	Red	K	for	blacK
G	for	Green	N	for	browN
P	for	Purple	E	for	bluE
Y	for	Yellow	O	for	Orange

Idea Book for Cuisenaire® Rods at the Primary Level   © Learning Resources, Inc.

WORKSHEET ON COLORING ROD LENGTHS 1

Grades: K, 1, 2

Name: _____ Date: _____

Find the rod that matches each train of white rods. Color the length with the correct rod color.

① 9W

② 2W

③ 5W

④ 10W

⑤ 3W

⑥ 8W

⑦ 4W

⑧ 7W

⑨ 6W

W	for	White	D	for	Dark Green
R	for	Red	K	for	blacK
G	for	Green	N	for	browN
P	for	Purple	E	for	bluE
Y	for	Yellow	O	for	Orange

© Learning Resources, Inc. Idea Book for Cuisenaire® Rods at the Primary Level

WORKSHEET ON COLORING ROD LENGTHS 2

Grades: K,1,2

Name: Date:

Find the rod that matches each train of white rods. Color the length with the correct rod color.

① 8W

② 3W

③ 5W

④ 7W

⑤ 6W

⑥ 10W

⑦ 2W

⑧ 9W

⑨ 1W

W	for	White	D	for	Dark Green
R	for	Red	K	for	blacK
G	for	Green	N	for	browN
P	for	Purple	E	for	bluE
Y	for	Yellow	O	for	Orange

Grades: 1, 2

MATCHING CODES AND LENGTHS

Materials:
Worksheet on Matching Codes and Lengths, page 48
Cuisenaire® Rods for each child
Crayons matching the rod colors

Settings:
One child working individually
A small group, children working individually
A whole class, children working individually

Learning Experience:

The Worksheet on page 48 encourages the reverse thought process from the Worksheets on pages 45 and 46. Children look at the letter code, say the color name, think of the number of white rods equivalent to the rod length, and then color the correct length. Children should then check their answers with the rods.

Some children may need to use the rods to color the length correctly. Other students will use the rods to check answers but not to solve the problems. Many will be able to do this activity with proficiency. If the codes give trouble, especially K, E, and N, review how the codes were chosen (i.e., the last letter of the three words beginning with b, blacK, bluE and browN). If mastery is not obtained, it is fine to move on to give more practice within the context of rod stories being changed to number stories.

Worksheet Answer Key

Code	Name	# of White Rods
1. R	Red	2 W
2. P	Purple	4 W
3. O	Orange	10 W
4. K	Black	7 W
5. N	Brown	8 W
6. E	Blue	9 W
7. Y	Yellow	5 W
8. G	Green	3 W
9. D	Dark Green	6 W

Matching Codes and Lengths, page 48

Underlying Mathematics Related to NCTM Standards:
Association with rods and codes
Association of colors with lengths
Representation of lengths in terms of white rods
Counting from 1 to 10
Reasoning and proof

W	for White	D	for Dark Green
R	for Red	K	for blacK
G	for Green	N	for browN
P	for Purple	E	for bluE
Y	for Yellow	O	for Orange

© Learning Resources, Inc.

Idea Book for Cuisenaire® Rods at the Primary Level 47

Grades: 1, 2

WORKSHEET ON MATCHING CODES AND LENGTHS

Name: Date:

1. Look at the rod color below, and color the correct length of it using the correct rod color.
2. Record the number of white rods that match the rod.
3. Check your answers with the rods.

❶ R
_____
Number of white rods

❷ P
_____
Number of white rods

❸ O
_____
Number of white rods

❹ K
_____
Number of white rods

❺ N
_____
Number of white rods

❻ E
_____
Number of white rods

❼ Y
_____
Number of white rods

❽ G
_____
Number of white rods

❾ D
_____
Number of white rods

W	for	White	D	for	Dark Green
R	for	Red	K	for	blacK
G	for	Green	N	for	browN
P	for	Purple	E	for	bluE
Y	for	Yellow	O	for	Orange

Idea Book for Cuisenaire® Rods at the Primary Level   © Learning Resources, Inc.

SINGING ABOUT RODS AND NUMBERS

Grades: K,1,2

Materials:
Cuisenaire® Rods for the teacher

Settings:
Ten or more children led by the teacher

Learning Experience:
Give each child a Cuisenaire Rod so that all 10 colors are used, repeating the colors if there are more than 10 children. Review with children the number of white rods needed to match each rod: 1 red = 2 whites, 1 green = 3 whites, 1 purple = 4 whites, etc.

Lead the children in singing the adaptation of the song, "Oh When the Saints Come Marching In." When a particular color is mentioned, the children with the corresponding rod color stand up and march around, holding the rod in front of them. As soon as all 11 verses for the 10 colors have been sung, end with the chorus.

Chorus: Oh when the rods come marching through
            Oh when the rods come marching through,
            We can measure all the colors
            When the rods come marching through.

Verse 1:   First there is white. Let it be one
            First there is white, and it is one
            It's the first rod to march in
            Here is white, and it is one.

Verse 2:   Then there is red, and it is two
            Then there is red, and it is two
            It's the next rod to march in
            Here is red, and it is two.

Verse 3:   Then there is green, and it is three
            Then there is green, and it is three
            It's the next rod to march in
            Here is green, and it is three.

Verse 4:   Then there is purple, and it is four, etc.

Verse 5:   Then there is yellow, and it is five, etc.

Verse 6:   Then there is dark green, and it is six, etc.

Verse 7:   Then there is black, and it is seven, etc.

Verse 8:   Then there is brown, and it is eight, etc.

Verse 9:   Then there is blue, and it is nine, etc.

Verse 10:   Then there is orange, and it is ten
             Then there is orange, and it is ten
             It's the longest rod to march in
             Here's the orange, and it is ten.

Verse 11:   Now we are here
             All rods are here
             The Cuisenaire Rods are all here
             We have measured all 10 colors
             Numbers 1 through 10 are here.

Underlying Mathematics Related to NCTM Standards:
Representation of lengths in terms of white rods
Recognition of equivalencies of lengths
Association of sums with addends
Use of the equal sign
Meaning of addition
Use of addition sentences

Grades: 1, 2

CHANGING ROD STORIES TO NUMBER SENTENCES

Materials:
Worksheet on Changing Rod Stories to Number Sentences, page 51
Cuisenaire® Rods for each child
Pencil for each child
Crayons matching the rod colors for each child

Settings:
A small group led by the teacher
A whole class led by the teacher

Learning Experience:
Have children make a train with a red rod and a white rod. Ask them to find the single rod that matches and to write the plus story: R + W = G. Then, direct the children to match the rod answer with white rods. Now ask the children to describe the rod situation in terms of white rods: "2 white rods plus 1 white rod equals 3 white rods."

R	W		red + white
	G		green
W	W	W	white + white + white

2 + 1 = 3

The distinction is made in this Learning Experience between a plus story, which describes the situation with rods, and an addition sentence, which uses numerals to interpret the rod lengths in terms of white rods.

The Worksheet on page 51 marks the beginning of an extension of the rod work to more traditional arithmetic work. The children have carefully proceeded through all the developmental stages for the concept of addition. They have worked at the concrete level by manipulating rods to find the sum; at the pictorial level by coloring pictures of the rods; and now at the numerical level of writing an addition sentence with numbers.

The strip of graph paper helps make the transition from rods to numerals more apparent, since each grid is the length of one white rod. Hence, the arithmetic computation is a mere recording of a physical situation. The length of each rod involved in the addition process is expressed in terms of white rods.

Worksheet Answer Key

Changing Rod Stories to Number Sentences, page 51

| 1. 4 + 3 = 7 | 3. 6 + 4 = 10 | 5. 3 + 5 = 8 |
| 2. 1 + 5 = 6 | 4. 7 + 2 = 9 | 6. 5 + 5 = 10 |

Underlying Mathematics Related to NCTM Standards:
Representation of lengths in terms of white rods
Recognition of equivalencies of lengths
Association of sums with addends
Use of the equal sign
Meaning of addition
Use of addition sentences

WORKSHEET ON CHANGING ROD STORIES TO NUMBER SENTENCES

Grades: 1,2

Name: Date:

1. Color the train for each plus story.
2. Find and color the length that matches each train.
3. Write the number sentence.

W for White	D for Dark Green
R for Red	K for blacK
G for Green	N' for browN
P for Purple	E for bluE
Y for Yellow	O for Orange

1 P + G

_____ Number Sentence

2 W + Y

_____ Number Sentence

3 D + P

_____ Number Sentence

4 K + R

_____ Number Sentence

5 G + Y

_____ Number Sentence

6 Y + Y

_____ Number Sentence

Grades: K,1,2

FINDING SUMS

Materials:
Worksheet on Finding Sums, page 53
Worksheet Master for Sums on Differences, page 54
Cuisenaire® Rods for each child
Crayons matching the rod colors
Pencil for each child

Settings:
One child working individually
A small group, children working individually
A whole class, children working individually

Learning Experience:

The purpose of the Worksheet on page 53 is to relate numerals to the physical model of the rods. The ultimate use of the model is to provide a method for translating abstract math symbols into concrete representations. For a child, the concrete manipulation is eventually replaced by a mental visualization of that manipulation or by a pictorial representation of it.

It is important to go from numerals to rods and from rods to numerals to reinforce the addition facts being developed. Children will start to visualize the meaning of 2 + 3 equals 5. Repeated practice on worksheets like these is warranted. The Worksheet Master on page 54 is left open for you or the children to pose further problems.

At this stage of development, the sums should be kept less than or equal to the orange rod (10 white rods). Children can check their work using the

5 + 4	5 + 5
1 + 7	2 + 6
3 + 6	5 + 2
8 + 2	2 + 7
3 + 4	4 + 1

rods. More problems like the ones above should be given in conjunction with the Worksheet Master on page 54.

This would be a good time to introduce problems like 0 + 5 or 6 + 0 where taking no rod would represent the quantity of zero: 0+5=5 and 6+0=6.

Worksheet Answer Key
Finding Sums, page 53

1. 4 + 5 = 9 (purple + yellow = blue)
2. 6 + 2 = 8 (dark green + red = brown)
3. 7 + 1 = 8 (black + white = brown)
4. 8 + 2 = 10 (brown + red = orange)
5. 3 + 6 = 9 (green + dark green = blue)
6. 7 + 3 = 10 (black + green = orange)

Underlying Mathematics Related to NCTM Standards:
Representation of lengths in terms of white rods
Recognition of equivalencies of lengths
Association of sums with addends
Association of numbers with rods
Use of the equal sign
Meaning of addition
Use of addition sentences
Reasoning and proof

WORKSHEET ON FINDING SUMS

Grades: K, 1, 2

Name: _____ Date: _____

1. Look at the number story, and color a picture of a train to match it on the first gridline.
2. Color the second length that matches each train on the second gridline.
3. Complete the addition sentence.

① **4 + 5**

_____
Number Sentence

② **6 + 2**

_____
Number Sentence

③ **7 + 1**

_____
Number Sentence

④ **8 + 2**

_____
Number Sentence

⑤ **3 + 6**

_____
Number Sentence

⑥ **7 + 3**

_____
Number Sentence

© Learning Resources, Inc.

Grades: K, 1, 2

WORKSHEET MASTER FOR SUMS AND DIFFERENCES

Name: Date:

1. Write a rod story problem.
2. Color the rods for the story problem on the gridlines.
3. Write the complete rod story.

❶ _____

_____
Completed Rod Story

❷ _____

_____
Completed Rod Story

❸ _____

_____
Completed Rod Story

❹ _____

_____
Completed Rod Story

❺ _____

_____
Completed Rod Story

❻ _____

_____
Completed Rod Story

❼ _____

_____
Completed Rod Story

Idea Book for Cuisenaire® Rods at the Primary Level   © Learning Resources, Inc.

BUILDING AN ADDITION TABLE

Grades: 1,2

Materials:
Worksheet for Building an Addition Table, page 56
Cuisenaire® Rods for each child
Pencil for each child

Settings:
One child working individually
A small group, children working individually
A small group, children working in pairs

Learning Experience:

An addition table is a very compact way of showing the addition facts. It is made up of rows (going across in the horizontal direction) and columns (going down in the vertical direction). The addends are located on the left and top of the table. The sum of two addends goes in the box where the row and column of the two addends meet. At this stage of development, the table deals only with the facts where the sum is less than or equal to an orange rod (10 white rods). For the first table on page 56, the rods are stood on end in the box that represents the sum. When completed, it looks like a city with skyscrapers of ascending and descending heights. The rods used are indicated below by codes written in the appropriate boxes. In the second table on page 56, numerals are used for the addends and sums.

The addition table with rods show many patterns. These should be shared and discussed. Some important patterns include:
1. The entries in each row (or column) increase by 1 white rod as in a staircase.
2. Same rod colors lie on diagonals going from top right to the bottom left.

An addition table can also be shown with numerals. Similar patterns occur:
1. The entries in each row (or column) increase by 1.
2. Same sums lie on diagonals going from the top right to the bottom left.

Worksheet Answer Keys
Building an Addition Table, page 56

+	W	R	G	P	Y
W	R	G	P	Y	D
R	G	P	Y	D	K
G	P	Y	D	K	N
P	Y	D	K	N	E
Y	D	K	N	E	O

+	1	2	3	4	5
1	2	3	4	5	6
2	3	4	5	6	7
3	4	5	6	7	8
4	5	6	7	8	9
5	6	7	8	9	10

Underlying Mathematics Related to NCTM Standards:
Representation of lengths in terms of white rods
Association of sums with addends
Association of numbers with rods
Use of a table with rows and columns
Meaning of addition
Communication and verbalization of findings

W	for	White	D	for	Dark Green
R	for	Red	K	for	blacK
G	for	Green	N	for	browN
P	for	Purple	E	for	bluE
Y	for	Yellow	O	for	Orange

© Learning Resources, Inc.

Idea Book for Cuisenaire® Rods at the Primary Level

Grades: 1, 2

WORKSHEET FOR BUILDING AN ADDITION TABLE

Name: Date:

1. Choose a rod code from the left side of the table and a rod code from the top of the table to represent two addends.
2. Find the rod that represents the sum, and stand it on end in the box where the row and the column of the two addends meet.
3. Complete this activity for all boxes in this table. Look for patterns in the finished table.

+	W	R	G	P	Y
W					
R					
G					
P					
Y					

1. Choose a number from the left side of the table and a number from the top of the table to represent two addends.
2. Write the sum of the two numbers in the box where the row and column of the two addends meet.
3. Finish the rest of the table this way.
4. Look for patterns in the finished table.

+	1	2	3	4	5
1					
2					
3					
4					
5					

Grades: 1, 2

PRACTICING ORANGE PLUS STORIES

Materials:
Cuisenaire® Rods for each child

Settings:
A small group led by the teacher
A whole class led by the teacher

Learning Experience:

Once children have the facts to 10 well understood, it is important to expand to the facts to sums that are greater than 10. To start, ask the children to make a train with a blue rod and a purple rod and to match this train with a one-color white train. The children should then match this length with a two-car train consisting of an orange rod plus another rod. For example:

E									P			
W	W	W	W	W	W	W	W	W	W	W	W	W
O									G			

blue + purple

13 whites

orange + green

In terms of white rods, E + P represents 9W + 4W, or 13 whites. The 13 whites are equivalent to O + G. O + G can be thought of as 10 + 3. In other words, the rods have been used to model 9 + 4 =13. Children will relate this to their number work because this experience builds readiness for addition facts with sums larger than ten and for regrouping into tens and ones.

Some further examples of trains include:

black + yellow	yellow + black
brown + dark green	dark green + brown
blue + red	red + blue
dark green + yellow	yellow + dark green
black + brown	brown + black
blue + black	black + blue

Children should match each of these trains with a two-car orange plus train. When students seem ready, they can give the results in terms of number sentences. For example:

black + yellow = orange + red
7 + 5 = 10 + 2 = 12

brown + dark green = orange + purple
8 + 6 = 10 + 4 = 14

blue + red = orange + white
9 + 2 = 10 + 1 = 11

Underlying Mathematics Related to NCTM Standards:
Recognition of equivalencies of lengths
Representation of lengths in terms of white rods
Association of sums with addends
Counting from 1-20
Place value (tens and ones)
Readiness for tens and ones

W	for	White	D	for	Dark Green
R	for	Red	K	for	blacK
G	for	Green	N	for	browN
P	for	Purple	E	for	bluE
Y	for	Yellow	O	for	Orange

© Learning Resources, Inc.

Idea Book for Cuisenaire® Rods at the Primary Level

Grades: 1, 2

FINDING SUMS GREATER THAN 10

Materials:
Cuisenaire® Rods for each child
Pencil and Paper for each child

Settings:
A small group led by the teacher
A whole class led by the teacher

Learning Experience:

For further practice with sums greater than 10, ask the children to place a dark green and a black rod end-to-end. Observe that this length is greater than an orange rod. Ask the children to find the *orange plus* train that will match.

D	K
O	G

dark green + black
orange + green

Record the plus story using the rod codes: D + K = O + G

Now ask children to match these trains with white rods.

D	K
O	G
W W W W W W W W W W W W W	

dark green + black
orange + green
13 whites

Next, write the addition sentence on the chalkboard: 6 + 7 = 10 + 3 = 13

Children may use other patterns as well to check their sums. For example, 6 + 7 can be thought of as being 1 more than 6 + 6 or 1 less than 7 + 7. This is because children often remember the sums of doubles, 6 + 6, 7 + 7, 8 + 8, 9 + 9, and can relate other less familiar facts to these. The use of such patterns should be encouraged.

Have children practice matching each train below with a two-car orange plus train:

8 + 5 = ___   9 + 7 = ___   9 + 3 = ___
8 + 8 = ___   7 + 4 = ___   5 + 6 = ___

When students seem ready, they can give the results in terms of number sentences.

Underlying Mathematics Related to NCTM Standards:
Recognition of equivalencies of lengths
Representation of lengths in terms of white rods
Association of sums with addends
Counting from 1 to 20
Place value (tens and ones)
Readiness for tens and ones

Grades: 1, 2

USING NUMBER LINES TO ADD

Materials:
Worksheet on Using Number Lines to Add, page 60
Worksheet Master for Number Lines, page 61
Cuisenaire® Rods for each child
Pencil for each child

Settings:
One child working individually
A small group, children working individually
A whole class, children working individually

Learning Experience:

The placement of rods on a number line marked in centimeters is another method of representing numbers with the rods. Again the length of a white rod serves as a useful unit for the whole number work with addition.

The first addend is represented by a rod with its left edge at 0 (zero). The second addend is placed so that the rods are end-to-end in a rod train. The total length can be read directly from the number line at the right edge of the second addend.

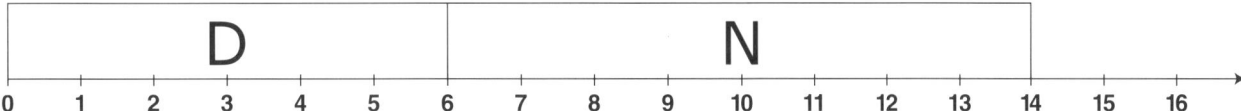

The rods provide a method that shows how two addends are two quantities that are placed on the number line. This is a more accurate method for many students than trying to hop "by ones" on a number line. For example, using the rods model, 6 + 8 is simply one six (dark green rod) and one eight (brown rod) with the train ending at 14. In contrast, using the "hopping" method, 6 + 8 is done as: start at 0, take 6 hops and then 8 hops to land at 14. If children seem ready to appreciate both methods, each can reinforce the other.

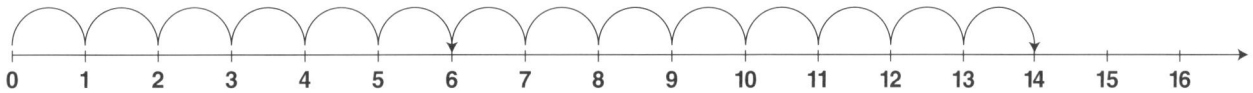

The number line approach used with rods provides a visualization of the abstract processes. The *Worksheet Master for Number Lines* on page 61 is open-ended for further practice as needed. Number Lines can be used for subtraction as well as addition. The method for subtraction will be described on page 76.

Underlying Mathematics Related to NCTM Standards:
Recognition of equivalencies of lengths
Representation of lengths in terms of white rods
Association of sums with addends
Counting from 1-20
Place value (tens and ones)
Readiness for tens and ones

W	for	White	D	for	Dark Green
R	for	Red	K	for	blacK
G	for	Green	N	for	browN
P	for	Purple	E	for	bluE
Y	for	Yellow	O	for	Orange

© Learning Resources, Inc.

Grades: 1, 2

WORKSHEET ON USING NUMBER LINES TO ADD

Name: Date:

1. Use your rods on the number lines to find the sums of each addition question below.
2. Complete the addition sentence.

EXAMPLE

3 + 5 | G | Y | 3 + 5 = 8
          0 1 2 3 4 5 6 7 8 9 10   Addition Sentence

❶   2 + 4
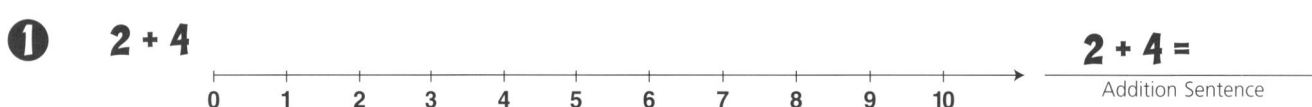
2 + 4 = ____
Addition Sentence

❷   8 + 1

8 + 1 = ____
Addition Sentence

❸   7 + 3
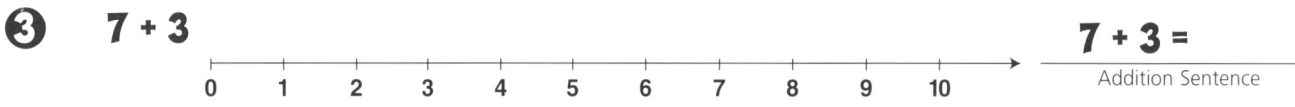
7 + 3 = ____
Addition Sentence

❹   4 + 6
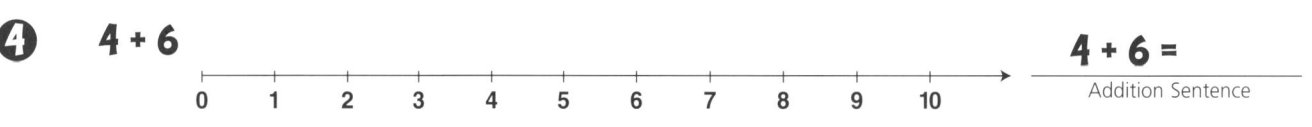
4 + 6 = ____
Addition Sentence

❺   1 + 5

1 + 5 = ____
Addition Sentence

❻   4 + 4
4 + 4 = ____
Addition Sentence

❼   3 + 6

3 + 6 = ____
Addition Sentence

Idea Book for Cuisenaire® Rods at the Primary Level   © Learning Resources, Inc.

WORKSHEET MASTER FOR NUMBER LINES

Grades: 1, 2

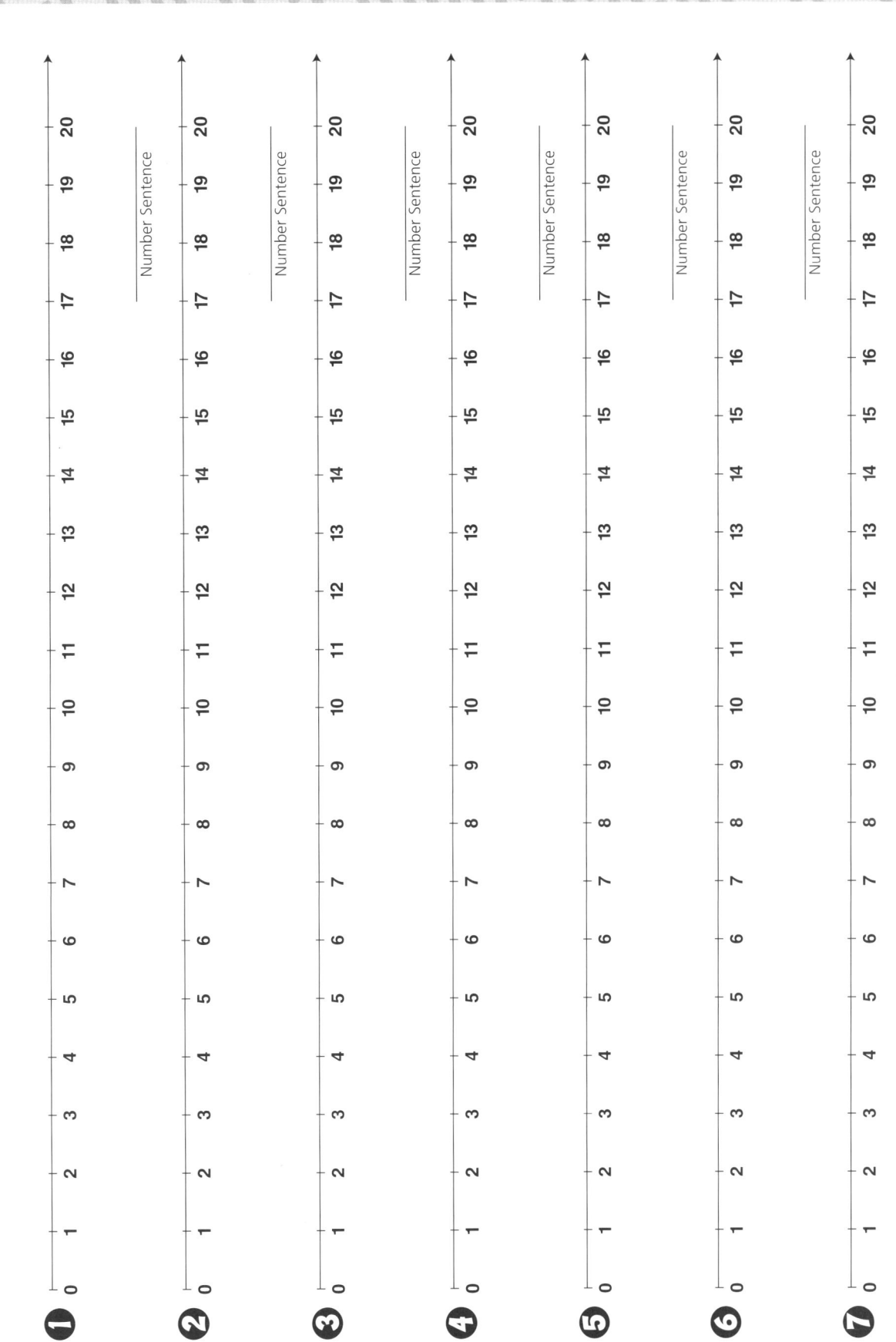

Grades: K, 1, 2

MAKING AN ADDITION TABLE WITH SUMS to 20

Materials:
Worksheet on Making an Addition Table, page 63
Cuisenaire® Rods for each child
Pencil for each child

Settings:
One child working individually
A small group, children working individually
A whole class, children working individually

Learning Experience:

By this time, the children can figure out all the addition facts from 1 + 1 to 10 + 10. This Learning Experience provides children with the opportunity to fill in an addition table that goes up to 20. (The addends are on the left side and top of the table, and the sum of two addends goes in the box where the row and column of the two addends meet.)

Children may need some help with where to place the answers. They also should check their sums with rods. Once this sheet is completed, have children keep it for reference while doing future addition and subtraction problems.

It is also helpful to have a large poster of the addition table for the bulletin board. Having the correct facts visible in the classroom helps the children learn them in much the same way that the posting of the upper and lower case letters has helped children with writing and printing. Plus, children will enjoy helping you make it.

Once this activity is complete, encourage the children to discuss the patterns in the table. This will help them relate the facts to one another and visualize all the combinations that result in the same sum.

Observing the common sums along the diagonals is important. This relates to the rod activity of finding all the two-car trains that match one particular rod length. For example, for the dark green rod, W + Y, R + P, G + G, P + R, and Y + W can be represented numerically by the facts 1 + 5, 2 + 4, 3 + 3, 4 + 2, and 5 + 1 all having the same sum of 6. This table will also be helpful with the upcoming work on missing addends and subtraction.

Worksheet Answer Key
Making an Addition Table, page 63

+	1	2	3	4	5	6	7	8	9	10
1	2	3	4	5	6	7	8	9	10	11
2	3	4	5	6	7	8	9	10	11	12
3	4	5	6	7	8	9	10	11	12	13
4	5	6	7	8	9	10	11	12	13	14
5	6	7	8	9	10	11	12	13	14	15
6	7	8	9	10	11	12	13	14	15	16
7	8	9	10	11	12	13	14	15	16	17
8	9	10	11	12	13	14	15	16	17	18
9	10	11	12	13	14	15	16	17	18	19
10	11	12	13	14	15	16	17	18	19	20

Underlying Mathematics Related to NCTM Standards:
Awareness of rod attributes (length, color, and shape)
Association of colors with rods
Recognition of equivalencies of lengths
Connections to life experiences
Communication and verbalization of ideas

Grades: 1, 2

WORKSHEET ON MAKING AN ADDITION TABLE

Name: Date:

1. Choose a number from the left side of the table and a number from the top of the table to represent two addends.
2. Write the sum of the two numbers in the box where the row and column of the two addends meet.
3. Finish the entire table this way.
4. Look for patterns in the finished table.

+	1	2	3	4	5	6	7	8	9	10
1										
2										
3										
4										
5										
6										
7										
8										
9										
10										

Use your rods to check the sums.

0 1 2 3 4 5 6 7 8 9 10 11 12 13 14 15 16 17 18 19 20

© Learning Resources, Inc.   Idea Book for Cuisenaire® Rods at the Primary Level

Grades: 1, 2

FINDING THE MISSING ROD

Materials:
Cuisenaire® Rods for each pair of children

Settings:
Two children working together
A small group, children working in pairs
A whole class, children working in pairs

Learning Experience:

This activity is the beginning of a sequence of concrete experiences with the concept of missing addends. Missing addends warrant a lot of attention and continued practice at the concrete level because they help children with arithmetic computation.

Ask student pairs to build all the two-car trains for the dark green rod, the black rod, the brown rod, the blue rod, and the orange rod. If the trains are made in staircase patterns, they may be easier for the children to see how one addend increases and the other decreases as a constant sum is maintained. The patterns should be discussed and related to the constant sums shown in the addition table on pages 62 and 63.

Ask one of the partners to close his or her eyes. The other partner removes one rod from the rod pattern for dark green. On a signal, the first partner opens his or her eyes and tries to guess the missing rod. Then the partners switch roles and play finding the missing rod from the black, blue, and orange patterns. This game of finding the missing rod lays foundations at the concrete level for later computational work.

Dark Green	Black	Brown	Blue	Orange
W + Y	W + D	W + K	W + N	W + E
R + P	R + Y	R + D	R + K	R + N
G + G	G + P	G + Y	G + D	G + K
P + R	P + G	P + P	P + Y	P + D
Y + W	Y + R	Y + G	Y + P	Y + Y
	D + W	D + R	D + G	D + P
		K + W	K + R	K + G
			N + W	N + R
				E + W

Underlying Mathematics Related to NCTM Standards:
Association of various addends for a sum
Association of codes with rods
Missing addends
Communication and verbalization of ideas

W	for	White	D	for	Dark Green
R	for	Red	K	for	blacK
G	for	Green	N	for	browN
P	for	Purple	E	for	bluE
Y	for	Yellow	O	for	Orange

Grades: 1, 2

PLAYING CHALLENGE MATCH GAME FOR MISSING ADDENDS

Materials:
Cuisenaire® Rods for each pair of children

Settings:
Two children working together
A small group, children working in pairs
A whole class, children working in pairs

Learning Experience:

This is a very helpful experience for children to practice missing addend problems. Gameplay starts by placing about 40-50 assorted rods in the center of the table for each student pair. The first player chooses two rods of different colors and places them side-by-side, so the long ends touch, as shown at right.

The second player must find the missing addend, or the rod that is added to the shorter rod so it matches the longer rod. The second player keeps the three rods involved in the match.

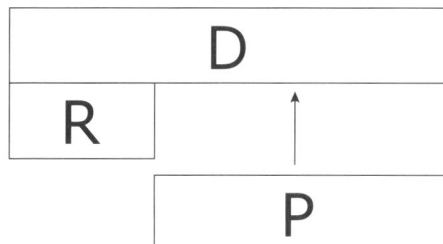

The partners reverse roles. As the game continues, the pile of rods in the center of the table gets smaller and smaller. The object of the game is to make a challenge that cannot be matched with the remaining rods. The player to do this first wins the game and scores one point for each rod left in the center of the table. Score may be accumulated from game to game.

This game is a precursor to subtraction. The same rod configuration above can be considered as a representation of a missing addend situation, red + _____ = dark green or a subtraction situation dark green – red = _____. In both cases the missing rod is the purple rod.

This game is enjoyable for children to play during free time and need not be played during scheduled mathematics time. They may wish to alternate this version of Challenge Match with the Challenge Match Game for Addends described on page 29.

Underlying Mathematics Related to NCTM Standards:
Awareness of rod attributes (length, color, and shape)
Association of colors with rods
Recognition of equivalencies of lengths
Connections to life experiences
Communication and verbalization of ideas

W	for	White	D	for	Dark Green
R	for	Red	K	for	blacK
G	for	Green	N	for	browN
P	for	Purple	E	for	bluE
Y	for	Yellow	O	for	Orange

© Learning Resources, Inc.

Grades: K, 1, 2

PLAYING THE I WISH I HAD GAME

Materials:
Cuisenaire® Rods for each child
Box or can (optional)
Crepe paper (optional)

Settings:
A small group led by the teacher
A whole class led by the teacher

Learning Experience:

Another fun activity for children to practice missing addends is the *I WISH I HAD* game. The leader picks up a rod and wishes for a longer rod. The goal is to find the rod that will make a train with the original rod to become equivalent to the wished for rod. For example, take a green rod in your hand. Tell the children:

> I have a green rod.
> I WISH I HAD a brown rod.
> Find the rod I need to make the train
>   as long as the brown rod.

Some children will need to try several rods before finding the correct answer. By trial and error, children can see that some rods are too long, some are too short, but one is "just right," that being the yellow rod. Some children start to make connections with subtraction: *If you took the length of a green rod away from the length of a brown rod, the length of a yellow rod would be left.*

Play *I WISH I HAD* for other rods. Do this activity many times, letting the children take turns to act as leader to tell the *I WISH I HAD* story. A silent version of the game can also be played by establishing ahead of time one of the longer rods as the WISH for a whole series of problems. The leader then holds up one rod at a time, and the other children hold up the rod that combines with the leader's rod to give the wished for length.

The fantasy of wishing is very motivating for children. It is also possible to decorate a box or can with crepe paper to make a wishing well. One child acts as leader and tosses a rod into the well, while making a wish for a longer rod. Another child tells the missing addend story and checks the results by completing the rod train. Once the rod triple is made, the child can tell the rod story with color names. For example, *green plus yellow equals brown.* Then they can give the comparable number sentence (3 + 5 = 8) if this seems appropriate to their level of understanding.

Underlying Mathematics Related to NCTM Standards:
Recognition of equivalencies of lengths
Missing addends
Meaning of subtraction
Connections between missing addends and subtraction
Communication and verbalization of findings
Reasoning and proof

PLAYING CUISENAIRE® HOPSCOTCH

Grades: K, 1, 2

Materials:
One sheet of dark green, black, brown, blue, and orange construction paper
Masking tape
Cuisenaire® Rods for each group
Bag

Settings:
A small group, children working together
A whole class, children working in small groups

Learning Experience:

Tape one sheet of construction paper in each color to the floor or pavement in a T shape to form a Hopscotch mat. Place the corresponding rod in the upper left corner of the piece of paper of the same color.

Place two rods of each of the five colors into a bag: white, red, green, purple, and yellow. The children take turns reaching into the bag and choosing a rod.

On a turn, the player tosses the rod onto one of the squares on the mat. The player hops through the path on one or two feet.

When the player lands on the square with the two rods, the player must tell what rod should be combined with the smaller rod to make a train the same length as the longer rod. The player should actually match the rods to find the correct missing addend. If the player is correct, he or she finishes hopping through the path in both directions. The children may play as many rounds as they wish.

A more challenging version involves each child holding the rod chosen from the bag and hopping from square to square on one turn. When landing on each square, the child must name the rod that would combine with the rod in his or her hand to make a train the length of the rod on the square. For the first few games, children may need to match the rods to find the correct missing addends.

The goal is to be able to hop in both directions of the mat without a mistake. Note that the return trip provides the same missing addend problems, but in reverse order, and should act as reinforcement of the learning. The children may play as many rounds as they wish.

Underlying Mathematics Related to NCTM Standards:
Recognition of equivalencies of lengths
Missing addends
Connections between missing addends and subtraction
Communication and verbalization of findings
Reasoning and proof
Bodily-kinesthetic movements

Grades: 1, 2

SOLVING THE CASE OF THE MISSING ADDEND

Materials:
Cuisenaire® Rods for each child
An orange rod for each child
Orange construction paper
Scissors and transparent tape

Settings:
A small group, children working in pairs
A whole class, children working in pairs

Learning Experience:

Knowing missing addends for 10 is helpful for mental computation. For example, when adding 8 + 6, it is helpful to think about 8 needing 2 more to make 10. When the 2 is taken from the 6, this would leave 4. Hence 8 + 6 is equivalent to 10 + 4, giving the answer 14.

One way of helping students learn missing addends for 10 is to make an orange rod case. Each child should make an orange rod case out of orange construction paper. The orange construction paper should be cut the exact length of an orange rod (10 cm) and a width of about 5 cm. Then it is wrapped around an orange rod and taped together in order to make a loose fitting case the length of an orange rod. The children will enjoy making rod cases for other rods, using the correct color of construction paper and cutting it the correct length.

Then, the orange rod should be removed from the case and placed in the center of the table to serve as a frame of reference. Without letting the second player see, the first player fills the rod case exactly with two rods (a two-car train for orange). The first player then shows the second player one end of the rod case.

The second player interprets the situation using rods. For example: **brown + _____ = orange**

The second player calculates what the other rod is in the rod case, and is shown the other end of the rod case to see if the answer was correct. In the example above, brown + red = orange. Then the partners switch roles.

A more difficult version involves three addends to make a "rod sandwich." Without letting the second player see, the first player fills the rod case exactly with three rods. (A three-car train for orange.) The first player shows the second player the two ends of the rod case. The second player has to name the rod in the middle (the "filling" in the sandwich). The answer is checked, and the partners switch roles.

The player filling the rod case has to think about missing addends as much as the player guessing. Both players will find this activity fun and challenging.

Underlying Mathematics Related to NCTM Standards:
Recognition of equivalencies of lengths
Missing addends
Visual memory of shapes
Connections between missing addends and subtraction
Communication and verbalization of findings
Reasoning and proof

PRACTICING MISSING ADDENDS

Grades: 1, 2

Materials:
Worksheet Master for Sums and Differences, page 54
Cuisenaire® Rods for each child
Crayons matching the rod colors for each child
Pencil for each child

Settings:
One child working individually
A small group, children working individually
A whole class, children working individually

Learning Experience:
Photocopy and distribute three copies of page 54, and ask children to answer the following missing addend problems using the grids to check their work. The first set is to be given and completed with the color names:

green + _____ = yellow
white + _____ = brown
yellow + _____ = orange
red + _____ = dark green
blue + _____ = orange
green + _____ = blue
red + _____ = black

The next set is to be given and completed with the color codes:

W + _____ = O
R + _____ = Y
D + _____ = K
G + _____ = N
N + _____ = O
P + _____ = E
G + _____ = D

And finally give some problems as number sentences:

2 + _____ = 10
7 + _____ = 9
4 + _____ = 8
1 + _____ = 6
4 + _____ = 7
5 + _____ = 10
3 + _____ = 9

It should be noted that most children at this stage of development think of a missing addend situation as a missing piece in an addition problem. It is more sophisticated to realize that a subtraction technique can be used to find the missing length. The idea that addition and subtraction are inverse operations is very vividly shown with Cuisenaire Rod triples.

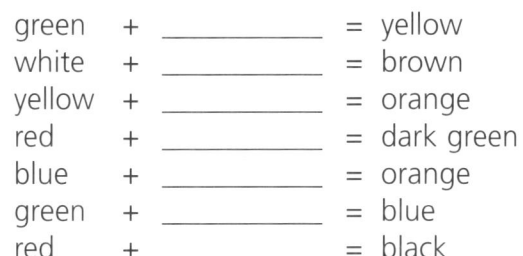

W	for	White	D	for	Dark Green
R	for	Red	K	for	blacK
G	for	Green	N	for	browN
P	for	Purple	E	for	bluE
Y	for	Yellow	O	for	Orange

Underlying Mathematics Related to NCTM Standards:
Recognition of equivalencies of lengths
Missing addends
Visual memory of shapes
Connections between missing addends and subtraction
Communication and verbalization of findings Reasoning and proof

© Learning Resources, Inc.
Idea Book for Cuisenaire® Rods at the Primary Level

SUBTRACTING BY FINDING HOW MUCH MORE

Grades: 1, 2

Materials:
Cuisenaire® Rods for each child
Cuisenaire® Rods for the teacher

Settings:
A small group led by the teacher
A whole class led by the teacher

Learning Experience:

Just as addition is shown by placing rods end-to-end, subtraction is shown by placing rods side-by-side. The rods show nicely that addition and subtraction are inverse operations.

To get started, ask the children to choose a yellow (Y) and a red (R) rod. Direct their attention to the difference in lengths between the two rods. Promote discussion by asking, *"How much more is the yellow rod than the red rod?"* The children must then find a rod that will combine with the red rod to make the length of the yellow rod. The answer is a green rod.

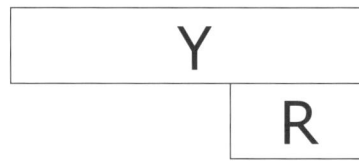 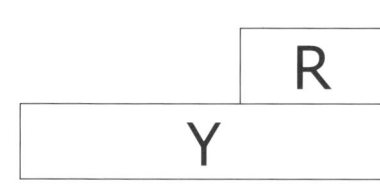 

Most children will sense that this way of viewing subtraction is similar to their work with missing addends. The rod configurations remain the same. All that has changed is the way of asking the question. The emphasis now is on the difference n length of two rods.

Work through several more examples with children, using the rods:
1. How much more is a black rod than a green rod? (answer: purple)
2. How much more is a blue rod than a purple rod? (answer: yellow)
3. How much more is an orange rod than a blue rod? (answer: white)
4. How much more is a dark green rod than a green rod? (answer: green)

Let the children give problems like these for their classmates to solve. It is important for children to verbalize the concepts in the form of a question to be interpreted with rods.

Underlying Mathematics Related to NCTM Standards:
Recognition of equivalencies of lengths
Visual memory of shapes
Missing addends
Meaning of subtraction
Connections between addition and subtraction
Communication and verbalization of findings
Reasoning and proof

Grades: 1,2

TEACHING SUBTRACTION AS TAKE AWAY

Materials:
Cuisenaire® Rods for each child
Cuisenaire® Rods for the teacher

Settings:
A small group led by the teacher
A whole class led by the teacher

Learning Experience:
Another way of looking at subtraction is the "take away" model. This can be demonstrated well with the rods. Choose two rods, such as a blue (E) and a purple (P) rod. Ask the children to imagine that an amount equal to the purple rod is "taken away" or "cut off" from the blue rod. This can be demonstrated by placing the purple rod beside or on top of the blue rod so that a yellow rod can match the portion of the blue rod showing.

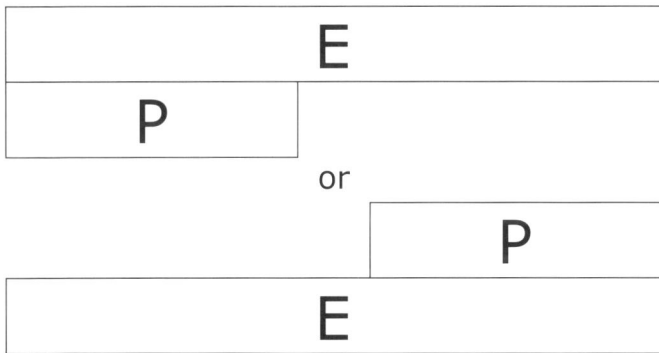

blue "take away" purple equals yellow

Try more "take away" problems using these rods

purple "take away" red (answer: red)
brown "take away" white (answer: black)
orange "take away" dark green (answer: purple)
blue "take away" red (answer: black)
dark green "take away" yellow (answer: white)

After this Learning Experience, children will have experienced three views of subtraction, as putting rods side-by-side for missing addends (page 65), as a "how much more" comparison (page 70), and as "take away." It is helpful to have more than one way to approach the concept of subtraction to meet individual differences and to provide reinforcement. You can create subtraction word problems to meet the three methods of subtraction.

1. **Missing addend**: John has 5 pencils and Jane has 2 pencils. How many more pencils does Jane need to have the same number as John?
2. **Difference comparison**: John has 5 pencils and Jane has 2 pencils. How many more pencils does John have than Jane?
3. **Take away**: John has 5 pencils and gave 2 to Jane. How many does John have left?

Underlying Mathematics Related to NCTM Standards:
Recognition of equivalencies of lengths
Visual memory of shapes
Missing addends
Meaning of subtraction

Connections between addition and subtraction
Communication and verbalization of findings
Reasoning and proof

Grades: 1, 2

INTRODUCING THE MINUS SIGN

Materials:
Worksheet Master for Sums and Differences, page 54
Cuisenaire® Rods for each child
Crayons matching the rod colors for each child

Settings:
A small group led by the teacher
A whole class led by the teacher

Learning Experience:

The Worksheet Master on page 54 has been left open-ended so you can give problems orally. The idea of placing rods side-by-side for subtraction should be well established before entering the pictorial stage of coloring rods on centimeter graph paper.

Describe each of the following subtraction situations orally. Have children color the appropriate rods on the graph paper strips and find the missing length. The word "minus" for subtraction should be introduced at this time.

orange "minus" red (answer: brown)
purple "minus" green (answer: white)
brown "minus" yellow (answer: green)
orange "minus" dark green (answer: purple)
black "minus" white (answer: dark green)
blue "minus" dark green (answer: green)
dark green "minus" purple (answer: red)

The minus sign can be used in the subtraction sentences as you write the following problems on the blackboard.

$$O - R = N \qquad P - G = W$$
$$N - Y = G \qquad O - D = P$$
$$K - W = D \qquad E - D = G$$
$$D - P = R$$

By observing you write and say the sentences, the children become more prepared for pages 73-77, which have children writing subtraction stories.

W	for	White	D	for	Dark Green
R	for	Red	K	for	blacK
G	for	Green	N	for	browN
P	for	Purple	E	for	bluE
Y	for	Yellow	O	for	Orange

Underlying Mathematics Related to NCTM Standards:
Recognition of equivalencies of lengths
Visual memory of shapes
Missing addends
Meaning of subtraction

Connections between addition and subtraction
Communication and verbalization of findings
Reasoning and proof

Grades: 1, 2

WRITING SUBTRACTION STORIES

Materials:
Worksheet on Subtraction Stories 1, page 74
Worksheet on Subtraction Stories 2, page 75
Worksheet Master for Sums and Differences, page 54
Cuisenaire® Rods for each child
Crayons matching the rod colors for each child
Pencil for each child

Settings:
One child working individually
A small group, children working individually
A whole class, children working individually

Learning Experience:

In this Learning Experience, subtraction problems are provided in the traditional arithmetic format. Have students use the Worksheets on pages 74 and 75 to look at each minus story and interpret it as two rods placed side-by-side. The rod lengths should then be colored on the strips provided.

The conversion to numerals comes from relating the value of each rod to white rods. First the child translates the minus story into numbers. Then he or she writes the completed subtraction sentence, using the rods as a self-checking device.

You or the children can pose more examples using the Worksheet Master on page 54. Children should be encouraged to interpret each problem with rods by coloring the rod picture to match the subtraction story. Once the difference is found and colored, they write the completed subtraction sentence. It is important to go from numerals to rods and from rods to numerals to reinforce the subtraction facts being developed. Repeated practice is warranted.

Worksheet Answer Keys

Subtraction Stories 1, page 74		Subtraction Stories 2, page 75			
1. 10 − 5	10 − 5 = 5	1. 6 − 2	6 − 2 = 4	6. 4	
2. 4 − 3	4 − 3 = 1	2. 7 − 4	7 − 4 = 3	7. 5	
3. 3 − 1	3 − 1 = 2	3. 9 − 8	9 − 8 = 1	8. 3	
4. 8 − 7	8 − 7 = 1	4. 10 − 7	10 − 7 = 3		
5. 9 − 4	9 − 4 = 5	5. 7 − 3	7 − 3 = 4		

It should be noted that the first number is larger than the second number in these subtraction problems. The rods can be used as a model for negative numbers, but not at this stage of development.

W	for	White	D	for	Dark Green
R	for	Red	K	for	blacK
G	for	Green	N	for	browN
P	for	Purple	E	for	bluE
Y	for	Yellow	O	for	Orange

Underlying Mathematics Related to NCTM Standards:
Association with numbers with rods
Use of subtraction sentences
Recognition of equivalencies of lengths
Connections between addition and subtraction
Meaning of subtraction
Use of the minus sign
Reasoning and proof

Grades: 1,2

WORKSHEET ON SUBTRACTION STORIES 1

Name: Date:

1. Color the subtraction story on the gridlines.
2. Write in the numbers to the right of the story.
3. Find the rod that matches the difference, and color that length on the second gridline.
4. Complete the subtraction sentence.

EXAMPLE

Y - G | Y | | | | | | 5 - 3
        | G | | | | | | 5 - 3 = 2

① O - Y

Subtraction Sentence

② P - G

Subtraction Sentence

③ G - W

Subtraction Sentence

④ N - K

Subtraction Sentence

⑤ E - P

Subtraction Sentence

WORKSHEET ON SUBTRACTION STORIES 2

Grades: 1,2

Name: _____ Date: _____

1. Color the subtraction story on the gridlines.
2. Write in the numbers to the right of the story.
3. Find the rod that matches the difference, and color that length on the second gridline.
4. Complete the subtraction sentence.

Subtraction Sentence

Subtraction Sentence

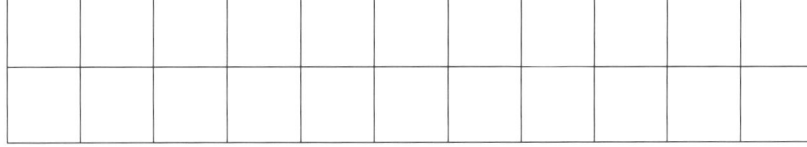

Subtraction Sentence

Subtraction Sentence

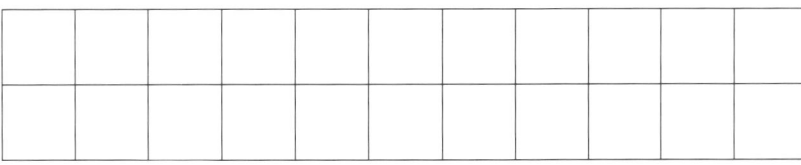

Subtraction Sentence

Try to solve these problems without using rods.

❻ 10 - 6 = ____   ❼ 9 - 4 = ____   ❽ 8 - 5 = ____

Grade: 2

USING NUMBER LINES TO SUBTRACT

Materials:
Worksheet for Number Line Subtraction, page 77
Worksheet Master for Number Lines, page 61
Cuisenaire® Rods for each child
Crayons matching the rod colors for each child
Pencil for each child

Settings:
One child working individually
A small group, children working individually
A whole class, children working individually

Learning Experience:
The number line model for subtraction involves placing the first rod with its left edge at 0. The second rod length is subtracted off by placing it on top of the first rod so that their right edges match. The difference between the two rods can be read directly from the number line, as shown below for yellow minus red or 5 – 2.

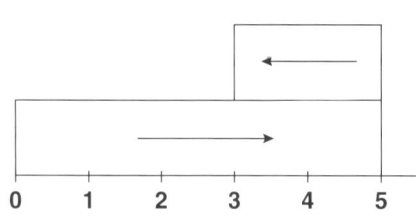

It should be noted that the number lines for rods should be gridded in centimeters since the numerical interpretation is in terms of white rods. Encourage children to do the subtraction problems on the Worksheet on page 77. After practice, you or the children can pose more problems on the Worksheet Master on page 61.

When the children are able to subtract well using numbers up to 10, they should then be encouraged to subtract using teen numbers where they will start with orange plus trains. Give them examples like:

18 – 9 Start with orange plus brown and subtract blue.
13 – 6 Start with orange plus green and subtract dark green.
20 – 7 Start with two orange rods and subtract black.
11 – 5 Start with orange plus white and subtract yellow.
17 – 7 Start with orange plus black and subtract black.
14 – 9 Start with orange plus purple and subtract blue.

The number line approach provides a visualization of the process of subtraction. Some children will find the use of number lines helpful. Not only can the number line with rods be used for subtraction, but it also shows the inverse relationship between addition and subtraction. For example, 5 – 2 = 3 is the inverse of 3 + 2 = 5.

Underlying Mathematics Related to NCTM Standards:
Association of numbers with rods
Recognition of equivalencies of lengths
Meaning of subtraction
Use of the minus sign

Use of subtraction sentences
Connections between addition and subtraction
Reasoning and proof

Idea Book for Cuisenaire® Rods at the Primary Level

© Learning Resources, Inc.

WORKSHEET FOR NUMBER LINE SUBTRACTION

Grade: 2

Name: _____ Date: _____

1. Use the rods on the number lines to find the difference between the two rods.
2. Then, write the completed subtraction sentence. Follow the example if you need help.

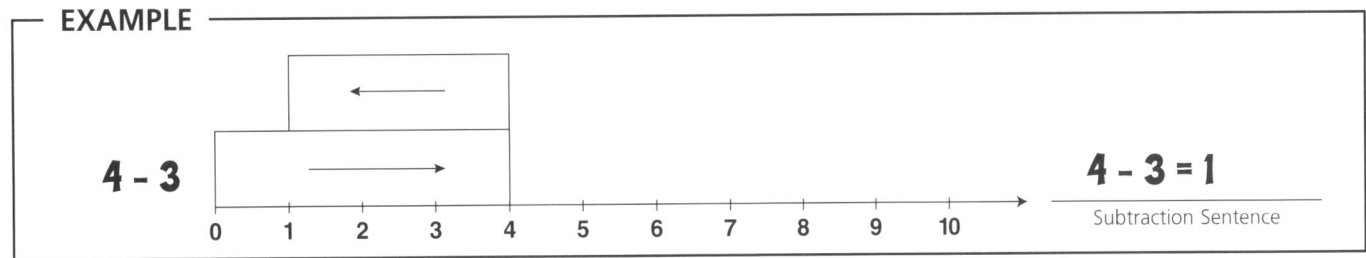

① 5 - 2

② 10 - 3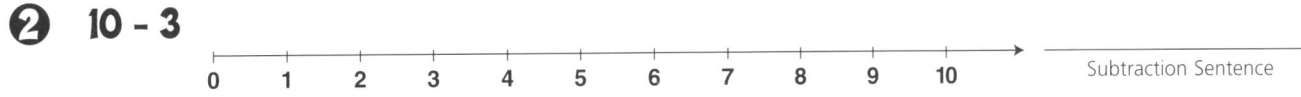

③ 7 - 1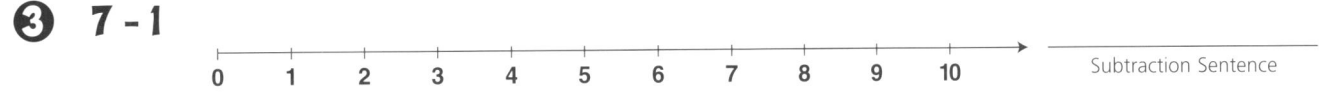

④ 6 - 3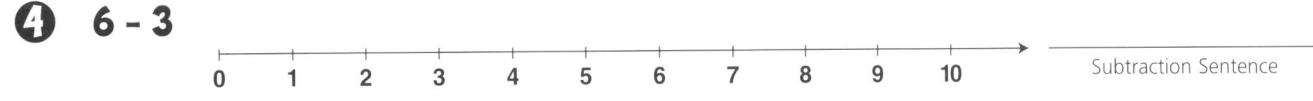

⑤ 9 - 2

⑥ 8 - 5

© Learning Resources, Inc.

Grade: 2

RELATING ADDITION AND SUBTRACTION STORIES

Materials:
Cuisenaire® Rods for each child
Paper and pencil for each child

Settings:
One child working individually
A small group, children working individually
A whole class, children working individually

Learning Experience:

All too often the focus on arithmetic practice problems is on the numbers involved rather than the operations described. If the first problem on the page is addition, children often do all subsequent problems as addition. This is natural, since in teaching the operations, we tend to treat each one separately. However, once the concepts have been established, children should have to deal with more than one process at a time.

A wonderful rod experience for children is to take the same three rods and to write their own addition and subtraction stories. The task should be kept light and enjoyable. The children should be encouraged to write all the possible addition and subtraction stories once they realize that there are actually eight possible stories for each rod triple. There are four addition stories and four subtraction stories. It is important for them to realize that the single number can be on the left side of the equality sign. Equals means equivalence in either order.

For example, for the white, purple and yellow rod triple, the following addition and subtraction sentences are possible.

```
5 = 1 + 4        5 - 4 = 1
1 + 4 = 5        1 = 5 - 4
4 + 1 = 5        5 - 1 = 4
5 = 4 + 1        4 = 5 - 1
```

Here are some others. Have the children make the appropriate rod triples.

```
2 + 8 = 10      8 = 5 + 3       3 + 2 = 5       4 + 6 = 10      9 = 4 + 5
10 = 2 + 8      5 + 3 = 8       5 = 3 + 2       10 = 4 + 6      4 + 5 = 9
8 + 2 = 10      8 = 3 + 5       2 + 3 = 5       6 + 4 = 10      9 = 5 + 4
10 = 8 + 2      3 + 5 = 8       5 = 2 + 3       10 = 6 + 4      5 + 4 = 9
10 - 2 = 8      8 - 3 = 5       5 - 3 = 2       10 - 4 = 6      9 - 4 = 5
8 = 10 - 2      5 = 8 - 3       2 = 5 - 3       6 = 10 - 4      5 = 9 - 4
10 - 8 = 2      8 - 5 = 3       5 - 2 = 3       10 - 6 = 4      9 - 5 = 4
2 = 10 - 8      3 = 8 - 5       3 = 5 - 2       4 = 10 - 6      4 = 9 - 5
```

Underlying Mathematics Related to NCTM Standards:
Association of numbers with rods
Recognition of equivalence of lengths
Use of addition sentences
Use of subtraction sentences
Inverse relationship between addition and subtraction

Grade: 2

HITTING THE TARGET NUMBER

Materials:
Worksheet Master for Number Lines, page 61
Cuisenaire® Rods for each child
Sixty index cards for each pair of children

Settings:
Two children working together
A small group, children working in pairs
A whole class, children working in pairs

Learning Experience:

This game may be played with rods and then with numbers.

Rod Version: Make a deck of 30 cards consisting of three cards for each of the 10 rod codes: W, R, G, P, Y, D, K, N, E, O.

Place the deck facedown between the partners. The partners agree on a target for the round; for example, two orange rods. On each turn, the player takes the top card from the deck and either adds or subtracts the value of the rod length in terms of white rods. As the game progresses, a player may go beyond the target value and then the other player will bring the value below the target by subtracting. The first player to hit the target exactly wins the game. The rods should be used to show each stage of the game. Often the students like to place the rods on a number line, such as those shown on the Worksheet Master on page 61.

Number Version: Make a deck of 30 cards consisting of three cards for each of the numerals: 1, 2, 3, 4, 5, 6, 7, 8, 9, 10. Place the deck facedown between the partners. The partners agree on a target number for the round; for example, 20. On each turn, the player takes the top card from the deck and chooses to add to or subtract from the value thus far in the game. The goal is to hit the target number exactly, as shown below.

1. Player 1:	5 "Add"	Value: 5	
2. Player 2:	9 "Add"	Value: 14	
3. Player 1:	8 "Add"	Value: 22	
4. Player 2:	3 "Subtract"	Value: 19	
5. Player 1:	4 "Add"	Value: 23	
6. Player 2:	5 "Subtract"	Value: 18	
7. Player 1:	2 "Add"	Value: 20	Target Number Winner!

After the children feel comfortable with one target number, increase that value appropriately.

Underlying Mathematics Related to NCTM Standards:
Association of rods with codes
Regrouping in addition
Regrouping in subtraction
Inverse relationship between addition and subtraction
Communication and verbalization of ideas

W	for	White	D	for	Dark Green
R	for	Red	K	for	blacK
G	for	Green	N	for	browN
P	for	Purple	E	for	bluE
Y	for	Yellow	O	for	Orange

Grades: 1, 2

PLAYING THE TRADING GAME FOR ADDITION

Materials:
Cuisenaire® Rods for each group
Extra white rods
One die for each group

Settings:
Two children working together
A whole class, children working in small groups

Learning Experience:

This game is closely related to the development of the concept of place value. As the children trade 10 white rods for 1 orange rod, they are building readiness for regrouping (carrying) in addition, where 10 ones are regrouped to one 10.

Choose one child in each group to be Banker. The Banker does not play the game, but is in charge of the rods. The Banker makes a staircase to remind players throughout the game of each rod length in terms of white rods.

The child on the Banker's left starts the game. The player tosses the die and asks the Banker for that number of white rods. Then the player trades the whites for a single rod of the same length.

On each turn, other than the first, the player combines the new rod with those already accumulated so that at the end of each turn, a player may have only one rod other than orange rods.

For example:

If a player has accumulated 2 orange rods and a blue rod and then tosses a six on the dice, the player would ask the Banker for 6 whites and trade them for a dark green. The player then combines the dark green and the blue for an orange plus yellow. At the end of the turn, the player has 3 orange rods and 1 yellow rod.

The first player to accumulate exactly 4 orange rods wins the game. A player may have to wait for the correct toss to end with exactly 4 orange rods. This delay allows other players to catch up and makes the game more fun. The probability of getting a particular value on a single (fair) die is one-sixth.

Children will enjoy playing this game many times throughout the year. After mastering this game, some children may want to use two dice, take the sum, get that many white rods and trade for a single rod (or orange plus white or orange plus red). The goal could be extended to 10 orange rods.

Underlying Mathematics Related to NCTM Standards:
Representation of lengths in terms of white rods
Recognition of equivalencies of lengths
Association of sums with addends
Regrouping in addition
Readiness for place value
Communication and verbalization of findings
Place value (tens and ones)
Introduction to probability

PLAYING THE TRADING GAME FOR SUBTRACTION

Grade: 2

Materials:
Cuisenaire® Rods for each group
Extra white rods
One die for each group

Settings:
A small group, children working together
A whole class, children working in small groups

Learning Experience:

This subtraction game should not be played until the basic *Playing the Trading Game for Addition* on page 80 has been experienced and well mastered. The idea of the equivalence of 10 white rods and 1 orange rod needs to be well established. In this subtraction game, the children pay back the value of the toss on the die rather than getting the value to keep, as they did in the addition game.

Choose one child in each group to be the Banker. The Banker does not play the game, but is in charge of the rods. The Banker makes a staircase to serve as a visual reminder throughout the game of the rod relationships.

Each player is given three orange rods at the start of the game. The child on the Banker's left takes the first turn. The player tosses the die and returns to the Banker a rod that is the same length as that number of white rods. The player may have to make trades with the Banker in order to "pay back" the correct rods.

For example:
If the first player tosses a two on the die, the player could trade one orange rod for a red rod plus a brown rod. The red rod is paid to the Banker, and the player ends the turn with 2 orange rods plus a brown rod.

The first player to pay back all the rods wins the game. Toward the end of the game, a player may have to wait several turns for the exact toss in order to get rid of the last rod.

As with the *Playing the Trading Game for Addition*, children will enjoy playing this game several times throughout the year. They may wish to change the starting value to four orange rods and then five orange rods. Children may also wish to alternate the addition game with the subtraction game. Encourage them to make up their own rules to alternate addition turns and subtraction turns.

Underlying Mathematics Related to NCTM Standards:
Recognition of equivalencies of lengths
Regrouping in addition
Regrouping in subtraction
Readiness for place value
Place value (tens and ones)
Communication and verbalization of findings
Introduction to probability

Grades: 1, 2

GENERATING MULTIPLES FROM ONE-COLOR TRAINS

Materials:
Cuisenaire® Rods for each child
Meter stick (optional)
Extra white rods for each child
Cuisenaire® Rods for the teacher

Settings:
A small group led by the teacher
A whole class led by the teacher

Learning Experience:

Ask the children to make a one-color train using only yellow (Y) rods. Increase the length of the train by one yellow at a time, making the train longer and longer. A meter stick, or a 50- or 25-cm ruler will help the child line up the cars of the train.

Once the train has about five or six cars, ask the children to match the train with white rods. Count the white rods with the children. Emphasize the number associated with the end of each yellow rod as being the same as the number of white rods needed at each stage.

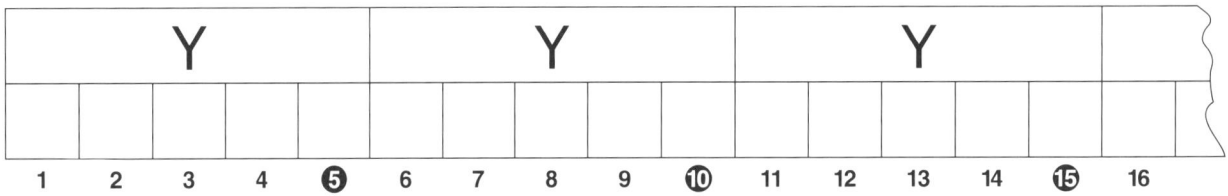

Read off the values at the ends of the yellow rods: 5, 10, 15, 20, etc. If a meter stick is used, this is an easy way for children to learn the multiples of five. Eventually the sequence of multiples of five might be remembered. However, mastery is not expected at this stage of the development. Repeat the same activity making a one-color train with orange rods so that multiples of 10 are generated (10, 20, 30, etc.).

When children are ready, try making a one-color red train to generate multiples of two, also known as the even numbers (2, 4, 6, 8, 10, etc.). Then you can move into the use of other one-color trains (green for multiples of three, purple for multiples of four, etc.). This work builds readiness for the multiplication facts.

Underlying Mathematics Related to NCTM Standards:
Representation of lengths in terms of white rods
Readiness for multiplication
Multiples of five
Multiples of 10
Multiples of two (even numbers)

FINDING FACTORS FROM ONE-COLOR TRAINS

Grade: 2

Materials:
Cuisenaire® Rods for each child
Cuisenaire® Rods for the teacher

Settings:
A small group led by the teacher
A whole class led by the teacher

Learning Experience:

Ask the children to take a dark green rod and to match it with train cars that are all the same color. The one-color trains for dark green are: 1 dark green, 2 greens, 3 reds, and 6 whites.

Since a dark green rod can be matched by a one-color train of red rods, red is called a factor of dark green. The set of factors for dark green are dark green, green, red, and white. This can also be thought of in terms of numbers. If the white rod is considered to be 1, the set of factors for 6 is 6, 3, 2, and 1. Each of the factors of a number divide into it leaving no remainder.

The term factor is not important for the children at this stage in the development, but the concept of one-color trains interpreted in this way lays the groundwork for division, factors, prime numbers, and fractions.

It is the factor and multiple relationships that led to the choice of color for each rod. To promote discussion, ask students the following questions:

1. What one-color train matches every rod? (white) (White is the presence of all color in the color spectrum and 1 is the only number that is a factor of all counting numbers.)

2. Which rods have only 2 one-colored trains? (red, green, yellow, and black) (These are the prime numbers that have only 1 and the number itself as factors.)

3. Which rod has only white and itself as factors and has no other multiple within the set of ten rods? (7 is the only prime number that doesn't also have a multiple in the set of 10 rods. The next multiple of 7 would be 14. Black is also the absence of all color in the color spectrum.)

The green rod is related to the dark green rod and the blue rod, since 3 is a factor of 6 and 9. The red rod is related to the purple rod, the dark green rod, the brown rod, and the orange rod since 2 is a factor of 4, 6, 8, and 10. The yellow rod is related to the orange rod since 5 is a factor of 10.

Underlying Mathematics Related to NCTM Standards:
Readiness for factors
Readiness for division
Readiness for prime numbers

FINDING HALVES

Grades: 1, 2

Materials:
Cuisenaire® Rods for each child
Cuisenaire® Rods for the teacher

Settings:
A small group led by the teacher
A whole class led by the teacher

Learning Experience:

Ask each child to take one rod of each of the 10 colors. Challenge the children to check each rod to see if it can be matched with a one-color train with two cars.

Since two white (W) rods match one red (R) rod, a white rod can be described as one-half of a red rod. Ask the children to describe the relationship for the other rods that can be matched with a one-color train with two cars.

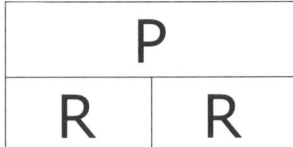

A red (R) is one-half of a purple (P) rod.

A green (G) rod is one-half of a dark green (D) rod.

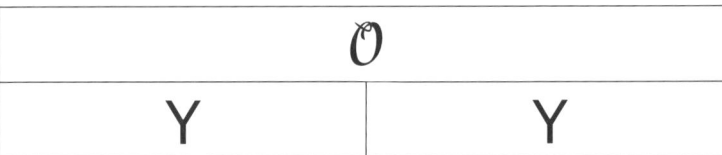

A purple (P) rod is one-half of a brown (N) rod.

A yellow (Y) rod is one-half of an orange (O) rod.

This experience helps children see one-half as a relationship rather than a fixed quantity. In terms of numbers with a white rod equaling the number 1, these rod relationships can be interpreted as 1 is one-half of 2, 2 is one-half of 4, 3 is one-half of 6, 4 is one-half of 8, and 5 is one-half of 10.

Children can find one-half relationships for orange plus trains as well. They will see, for example, that a dark green rod is one-half of orange plus red; in numbers, this can represent 6 as one-half of 12.

Underlying Mathematics Related to NCTM Standards:
Readiness for fractions
Association of numbers with rods
Communication and verbalization of findings
Seeing rods as relationships

INTERPRETING ONE-COLOR TRAINS AS FRACTIONAL PARTS

Grade: 2

Materials:
Cuisenaire® Rods for each child
Cuisenaire® Rods for the teacher

Settings:
A small group led by the teacher
A whole class led by the teacher

Learning Experience:

In this Learning Experience, the purple rod is going to be considered as having the value of one, so that fractional parts can emerge in another way. Start by asking the children to build all the one-color trains to match the purple.

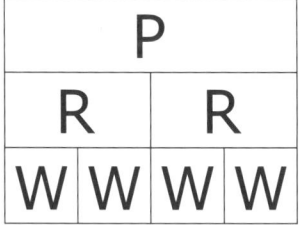

Since two red (R) rods match the purple (P) rod, each red rod is described as one-half of the purple rod. The rod configuration also shows that two halves make a whole (or one). Since four white (W) rods match the purple rod, each white rod is described as one-fourth of the purple rod. The rod configuration shows that one-half is equivalent to two-fourths and that four-fourths makes a whole (or one).

Now ask the children to build all the one-color trains to match the dark green rod, and let the dark green rod be considered as having the value of one.

Since two green (G) rods match the dark green (D) rod, each green rod is one-half the dark

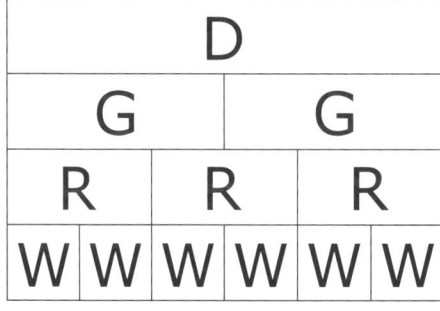

green rod. Similarly, each red (R) rod is one-third the dark green rod and each white (W) rod is one-sixth the dark green rod. It can be seen that three-sixths equals one-half, and that two-sixths equals one-third.

Ask the children to find a rod relationship for tenths. (Since 10 white rods match one orange rod, a white rod is one-tenth of an orange rod. The value of the rods in the staircase becomes one-tenth, two-tenths, three-tenths, etc.) Then ask the children to build all the one-color trains to match the brown rod and to describe the fractional parts that emerge (halves, fourths, and eighths).

Underlying Mathematics Related to NCTM Standards:
Readiness for fractions
Association of numbers with rods
Seeing rods as relationships
Letting rods other than white represent the value of one
Communication and verbalization of findings

Grades: K, 1, 2

PLACING RODS IN A PATTERN

Materials:
1-cm Graph Paper Master, page 15
Cuisenaire® Rods for each child
Cuisenaire® Rods for the teacher

Settings:
A small group led by the teacher
A whole class led by the teacher

Learning Experience:

As the children watch, stand some rods on end on the table to form a pattern, such as black, orange, black, orange, black, etc. Then, ask the children to observe the pattern, but not to verbalize it. The children show their awareness of the pattern by coming up and placing the next rod in the sequence. As more and more rods are placed, more and more children become aware of the pattern being used.

Ask for a volunteer to describe the pattern, and have all the children say the rod sequence in unison. Now, place the same rods in a train of alternating black and orange rods and see if the children can still say the sequence of colors as one of the children touches each rod in order from left to right. Then, stack the rods and see if the children can still see the pattern.

More advanced patterns should be used when the children seem ready. For example:

red, dark green, orange, red, dark green, orange, red, ...
purple, white, white, purple, white, white, purple, ...
green, yellow, green, orange, green, yellow, ...

Ask children what rod comes next for each case. Also see if the children can extend the patterns to the left as well as to the right by asking, "What rod comes before?" It helps children to see the pattern if the color names are said in the rhythm of the pattern and if a slight break is made between segments of the rod pattern.

You'll see that children will enjoy making patterns and sharing them with their classmates to extend in both directions. Some children may want to color rod patterns on graph paper. The pictures can be used later without rods to give children a more abstract experience of continuing a pattern.

Underlying Mathematics Related to NCTM Standards:
Association of colors with rods
Sequences of rod patterns
Logical thinking
Communication and verbalization of findings

MAKING RECTANGULAR PATTERNS

Grades: 1, 2

Materials:
1-cm Graph Paper Master, page 15
Cuisenaire® Rods for each pair
Cuisenaire® Rods for the teacher
Extra white rods

Settings:
A small group led by the teacher
A whole class led by the teacher

Learning Experience:

Challenge each pair of children to take six white rods, make a rectangle that is 2 x 3, and draw around it on 1-cm graph paper. Then have them form the other three rectangles that are possible to make with 6 white rods and draw around each of them.

Making rectangles is another way of looking at the factors of a number. The factors of 6 are 1, 2, 3, and 6. These are the possible dimensions of rectangles that can be formed using six white rods. The area of each of these rectangles is 6 square units (or 6 square centimeters for the rod model).

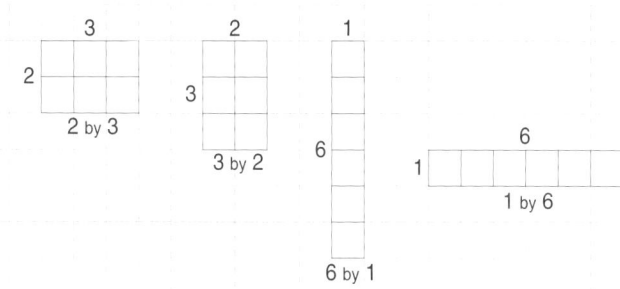

Since 6 has factors other than 1 and 6, it is called a composite number. For contrast, have the children take 7 white rods and build all the possible rectangles. Since the only rectangles that can be made have dimensions 1 by 7 or 7 by 1, the only factors of 7 are 1 and 7. Whenever a number has only 1 and itself as factors, it is known as a prime number.

Children can verify that 4, 6, 8, 9, 12, 15, 16, 18, and 20 are examples of composite numbers. Have the children make and draw around the various rectangles that they can make using the designated number of white rods. (Note that the number 1 is not considered prime or composite since the only factor of 1 is 1.)

This activity can also lead to some pre-multiplication thinking. The dimensions of each rectangle multiplied together gives the area (i.e., the number of squares that make up the rectangle drawn on the centimeter graph paper). This activity can also relate to pre-division work. If the child tries to make a rectangle out of 11 white rods where one of the attempted dimensions is 2, the results look like this:

A 2 by 5 rectangle is made but there is one white rod remaining. In other words, 2 divides into 11, 5 times with remainder 1.

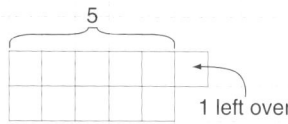

Underlying Mathematics Related to NCTM Standards:
Rectangular patterns
Composite and prime numbers
Counting
Concept of area

Communication and verbalization
  of findings
Pre-multiplication and -division
Reasoning and proof

COMBINING TWO STAIRCASES

Grades: K, 1, 2

Materials:
Cuisenaire® Rods for each child

Settings:
Two children working together
A small group, children working in pairs
A whole class, children working in pairs

Learning Experience:

Ask the children to build two identical staircases so that they fit together in some way. Two staircases may be combined in many creative ways. Share the various ways that children do it. Ask the children to try their partner's design or create a different one. See how many different ways your class can combine two staircases.

Some examples are given below:

A.
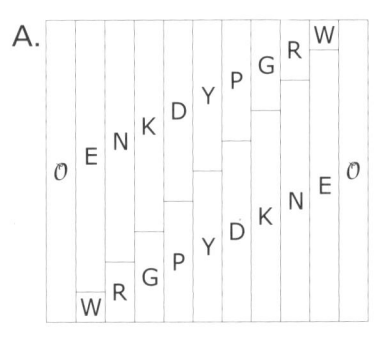

B.
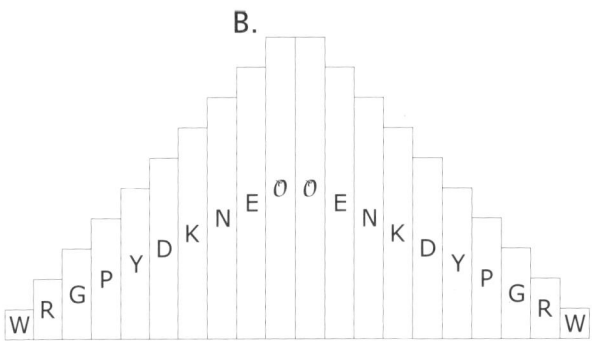

C.
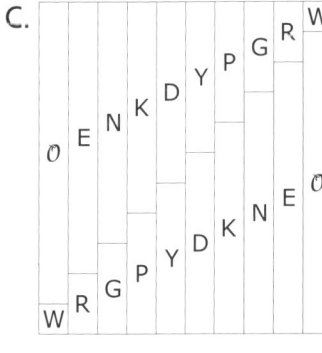

D.
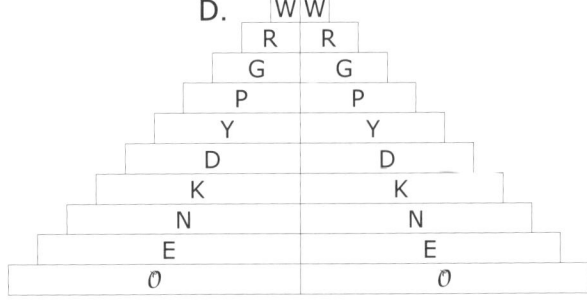

E.
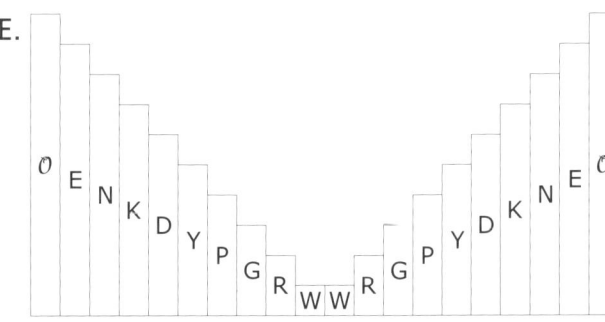

Children enjoy seeing the lines of symmetry in some patterns such as B., D., and E. Patterns A. and C. can be used to easily see that $1 + 2 + 3 + 4 + 5 + 6 + 7 + 8 + 9 + 10 = 55$. In each rectangle there are two staircase patterns and the total value can be viewed as 11 sums of 10 or 10 sums of 11, each totaling 110. Hence the total value of one staircase in terms of white rods is half of 110 or 55.

Underlying Mathematics Related to NCTM Standards:
Ordering of lengths
Logical thinking
Symmetry
Communication and verbalization of findings
Problem solving
Reasoning and proof

USING THE COMMUTATIVE PROPERTY OF ADDITION

Grades: 1, 2

Materials:
Cuisenaire® Rods for each child
Pencil and paper for each child

Settings:
A small group led by the teacher
A whole class led by the teacher

Learning Experience:

When children are asked to find all the two-car trains for the same sum, they should have a systematic approach to be sure that all the trains are found. For example, here are the patterns for the orange rod.

$O = W + E$
$O = E + W$
$O = R + N$
$O = N + R$
$O = G + K$

$O = K + G$
$O = P + D$
$O = D + P$
$O = Y + Y$

One approach is to build a train and then reverse the cars by means of the commutative property of addition. The commutative property is very important in arithmetic and algebra. It states that if the order of the two addends is reversed, the sum remains the same.

This method helps us to see some interesting patterns in the number of two-car trains. For example, the orange rod has an odd number of two-car trains since two rods of the same color match the orange rod. Here is a table showing the number of two-car trains for each rod except white. The number of two-car trains is one less than the length of the rod in terms of white rods.

Color of Rods	Number of Two-Car Trains
red	1
green	2
purple	3
yellow	4
dark green	5
black	6
brown	7
blue	8
orange	9

W	for	White	D	for	Dark Green
R	for	Red	K	for	blacK
G	for	Green	N	for	browN
P	for	Purple	E	for	bluE
Y	for	Yellow	O	for	Orange

Underlying Mathematics Related to NCTM Standards:

Recognition of equivalencies of lengths
Patterns and functions
Association of various addends for a sum
Reasoning and proof
Commutative property of addition

Grades: 1, 2

EXPLORING EVEN AND ODD NUMBERS

Materials:
Cuisenaire® Rods for each child
Pencil and paper for each child

Settings:
A small group led by the teacher
A whole class led by the teacher

Learning Experience:

Ask each child to build a staircase that starts with a red rod and "hops up" by a red (R) rod. The rods that will be used are red, purple (P), dark green (D), brown (N), and orange (O). This set of rods is called "the set of even rods."

This staircase is called an even staircase. Any rod that can be measured exactly by red rods is an "even" rod. If the white rod is considered as 1, the corresponding numbers in the even staircase are 2, 4, 6, 8, and 10. The staircase could be continued with orange plus red, orange plus purple, etc. to hop in even numbers beyond 10.

Ask the children to take the rods in an "even" staircase (red, purple, dark green, brown, orange) and to explore the property of "evenness" in another way. Have them show that each "even" rod can be matched exactly with two rods of the same color:

This activity builds readiness for the concept that every "even" number is twice another whole number. The rods that are not even are the white, green, yellow, black, and blue rods. These are called "odd." Have the children build the odd staircase and then show that none of the "odd" rods can be matched exactly with two rods of the same color. The corresponding numbers are 1, 3, 5, 7, 9, etc.

Red can be matched with 2 white rods.

Purple can be matched with 2 red rods.

Dark green can be matched with 2 green rods.

Brown can be matched with 2 purple rods.

Orange can be matched with 2 yellow rods.

Underlying Mathematics Related to NCTM Standards:
Recognition of equivalencies of lengths
Representation of lengths in terms of red rods
Counting from 1 to 10
Even and odd numbers
Even numbers as twice another number
Problem solving
Communication and verbalization of findings

Idea Book for Cuisenaire® Rods at the Primary Level © Learning Resources, Inc.

EXPLORING PATTERNS WITH SQUARE NUMBERS

Grade: 2

Materials:
1-cm Graph Paper for each child, page 15
Cuisenaire® Rods for each child
Extra white rods

Settings:
A small group led by the teacher
A whole class led by the teacher

Learning Experience:

Ask the children to take 4 white rods and place them on their 1-cm graph paper to form a square. Have them draw around this square. Explain that a square has the same length and width. The length and width are called the dimensions. The dimensions are 2 by 2.

Have them build the next size square, and ask, "How many white rods did it take?" (The answer is 9.) Have the children draw around this square. The dimensions are 3 by 3. Now, have the children build the next size square, and ask "How many white rods did it take this time?" (The answer is 16.) The dimensions for this square are 4 by 4 . Continue on, asking children to build the next size square to 25 and then 36 rods. The dimensions for a 36-rod square are 6 by 6. Once these are drawn, show the students that if you draw around one white rod, that would also be a square. The dimensions are 1 by 1. The set of 1, 4, 9, 16, 25, 36 ... is known as the set of square numbers.

Now ask the students to go back to their drawings to see that each square number is the sum of odd numbers. For example:

1+3=4 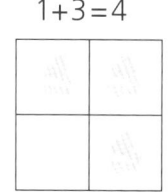   1+3+5=9

Children will enjoy discussing these patterns with each other. They may find other interesting patterns as well. For example, the number of odd numbers is the same as the length and width of the square.

Dimension	Number of White Rods
1 by 1	1
2 by 2	4
3 by 3	9
4 by 4	16
5 by 5	25
6 by 6	36

Underlying Mathematics Related to NCTM Standards:
Counting
Dimensions of a square (length, width)
Square numbers
Odd numbers

Patterns
Problem solving
Communication and verbalization of findings

Grades: 1, 2

PLAYING CUISENAIRE® ROD MANCALA

Materials:
White Cuisenaire® Rods for each child
Mancala Mat, page 93

Settings:
Two children working together
A small group, children working in pairs
A whole class, children working in pairs

Learning Experience:

The objective of the Mancala game is to collect the most rods at the end of the game. This is a variation on an ancient African game played with pits dug in the ground and with pebbles as the playing pieces.

Place the Mancala mat between the two players. The six "pockets" in front of each player are the player's playing area. A capture pit is on each player's right. For the earliest game, place 3 white rods in each of the 12 pockets. Later games can start with 4, 5, or 6 white rods in each of the 12 pockets.

Player 1 starts the game by removing all the rods in any one of the pockets on that side of the mat and placing one rod in each pocket by starting with the next pocket to his or her right. The player's own capture pit is included as a space to place a rod. Rods placed in the player's own capture pit become the score at the end of the game.

If there are enough rods to go past the player's capture pit, continue placing them into the opponent's pockets. However, skip your opponent's capture pit if you have enough rods to go that far around.

Whenever the player's last rod on a turn ends in the player's own capture pit the player gets another turn. This is something good to plan ahead for strategy. Also, whenever the player's last rod ends in an empty pocket on either side, the player captures that rod and all the rods in the opposite pocket, and places them in his or her capture pit for score. This is the end of the turn. Player 2 now follows the same rules by placing rods in each pocket in the direction of the capture pit on his or her right.

Turns alternate. The game ends when all six pockets on one side of the mat are empty. The other player takes the remaining rods from his or her pockets and places them in his or her capture pit. The player who has the larger number of rods in the capture pit wins. If 3 rods were placed in each pit at the beginning of the game, the total of the two scores should be 36 whites. For four rods it would be 48 whites; for five rods, 60 whites; for six rods, 72 whites. Children should play this game many times to work out winning strategies.

Underlying Mathematics Related to NCTM Standards:
Counting
Logical reasoning and strategic planning
Patterning
Communication and verbalization of findings

MASTER FOR MANCALA MAT

Grades: 1,2

Player 1's Capture Pit

Player 2 →

Player 1 →

Player 2's Capture Pit

Grades: 1, 2

PLAYING ROD MANCALA WITH VALUES

Materials:
White, red, and green Cuisenaire® Rods for each child
Mancala Mat, page 93

Settings:
Two children working together
A small group, children working in pairs
A whole class, children working in pairs

Learning Experience:

Here is another version of Cuisenaire® Rod Mancala that is based on using rod values. This game requires some different strategies since the goal is to capture the highest value, not necessarily the most rods.

Place the Mancala Mat between the two players. Place 2 white rods and 1 red rod in each of the 12 pockets. Player 1 starts the game by removing all the rods in any one of the pockets on that side of the mat and placing one rod in each pocket starting with the next pocket to the right. The player's own capture pit is included as a space to place a rod. Rods placed in the capture pit become the score at the end of the game.

Capturing the most valuable rods is advantageous. If there are enough rods to go past the capture pit, the player should continue placing them into the opponent's pockets. However, he or she should skip the opponent's capture pit if there are enough rods to go that far around.

Whenever the last rod on a turn ends in the player's capture pit, that player gets another turn. (This is something good to plan for as winning strategy.) Also whenever a player's last rod ends in an empty pocket on either side of the board, that player captures that rod and all the rods in the opposite pocket, and can place them in his or her capture pit for score. This is the end of the turn. Player 2 then plays by the same rules, placing rods in the direction of the capture pit to his or her right.

Turns alternate. The game ends when all six pockets on one side of the mat are empty. The other player takes the remaining rods from his or her pockets and places them in his or her capture pit. The player who has the higher value wins. Red rods are worth 2 white rods. This version of the game gives children a chance to do skip counting by 2s as they figure out their scores.

For example: If a player captures 8 red rods and 9 white rods, they can skip count 2, 4, 6, 8, 10, 12, 14, 16, and then add 9 more to get 25. This player can anticipate the opponent's score since the total score is 48. The opponent's score would be 48 − 25 = 23. Also, the opponent would have the remaining rods (4 red rods and 15 white rods) and can count 2, 4, 6, 8 and add to a score of 15 more, giving 23.

An easier version could start with just 1 white and 1 red in each pocket (total score = 36). A harder version could start with 2 white and 1 green (total score = 60) or 1 white, 1 red, and 1 green in each pocket (total score = 72).

Underlying Mathematics Related to NCTM Standards:
Counting
Logical reasoning and strategic planning
Skip counting (by 2s or by 3s)
Patterning
Communication and verbalization of findings
Problem solving
Reasoning and proof

Grades: 1, 2

PLAYING MANCALA GOING ROUND AND ROUND

Materials:
White, red, and green Cuisenaire® Rods for each child
Mancala Mat, page 93

Settings:
Two children working together
A whole class, children working in pairs

Learning Experience:

Here is still another version of Mancala with some fun and different rules regarding how the rods are placed into the pockets and how captures are made. The children start by using three whites in each of the 12 pockets (total value = 36). Later games can be played by starting with 2 white rods and 1 green rod (total value = 60) or 1 white, 1 red, and 1 green (total value = 72). In each case, capturing the higher value is the goal.

Player 1 starts by removing all the rods in any one of the pockets on his or her side of the mat and placing one rod successively in each pocket starting with the next pocket to the right. The player's own capture pit is included as a space to place a rod. If the last rod ends in the player's own capture pit, the player gets another turn.

If the last rod ends in any non-empty pocket on the board, all the rods in that pocket are removed and dropped one rod at a time successively around the board. The player can choose whether to drop a rod into the opponent's capture pit, as it will count toward the opponent's score. The reason a player might choose to do this is if this increases the possibility of an advantageous capture.

Whenever a player's last rod lands in an empty pit on either side of the board, the player captures that rod and all of the rods in the opposite pit. Turns alternate. The game ends when all six pockets on one side of the mat are empty. The other player takes the remaining rods from his or her pockets and places them in his or her capture pit. Score is counted and the total of the two players' scores should equal the starting values.

Underlying Mathematics Related to NCTM Standards:
Counting
Logical reasoning and strategic planning
Skip counting (by 2s or by 3s)
Patterning
Communication and verbalization of findings
Problem solving
Reasoning and proof

Grades: 1, 2

MAKING CUISENAIRE® CODE WORDS

Materials:
Worksheet for Code Words, page 97
Worksheet Master for Rod Code Words, page 98
Cuisenaire® Rods for each child
Pencil for each child

Settings:
One child working individually
A small group, children working individually
A whole class, children working individually

Learning Experience:

You probably taught the rod codes previously as a shortcut for the color names. For example, R for red, G for green, W for white, etc. This Learning experience reinforces the rod codes as alphabet letters that can be used to spell words. Even with the limited number of letters, W, R, G, P, Y, D, K, N, E, and O, many words can be written.

Some children will be quicker at this activity than others. Those who don't know what rod matches a given number of white rods should make a train of white rods and find the rod that matches the train. After this practice, have the children work on the Worksheet on page 97. On this Worksheet, children are asked to write the code for the rod that matches each train of whites. The number of white rods is written algebraically before the letter W. For example, 9 W represents a train with 9 white rods end-to-end. Since this is equivalent to a blue rod, 9 W is matched with the letter E.

Children can be asked to do three other very educational tasks during this exercise:

Worksheet Answer Key

1. POD, total value = 20 W
2. ORE, total value = 21 W
3. WORD, total value = 19 W
4. GROWN, total value = 24 W
5. YOYO, total value = 30 W
6. WORRY, total value = 20 W

Code Words, Page 97

1. Find the total value of the word in terms of white rods. This gives children practice in adding more than two addends. They can check their sums by placing the rods along a number line or metric ruler.
2. Give the meaning of the word and use it in a sentence.
3. Create words using the 10 rod code letters, and then use the Master Worksheet on page 98 to fill in the appropriate number of white rods for each letter and make another puzzle sheet for classmates. This is for children who can spell with ease.

Consider using the following words on the Master Worksheet on page 98 for your students to try. Children will enjoy guessing which word is the most valuable in a list. It won't necessarily be the longest word.

Three-Letter Words		Four-Letter words		Five-Letter Words		Six-Letter Words	
key	red	gone	deer	penny	perky	depend	wonder
nod	dew	noon	open	error	power	energy	eggnog
one	won	need	know	prong	rodeo	proper	pepper
pep	dry	weed	pond	drown	wedge	ponder	
won							

Here are three seven-letter words for a further challenge: powdery, reorder, redwood.

Underlying Mathematics Related to NCTM Standards:
Representation of lengths in terms of white rods
Association of rods with codes
Association of codes with rods
Counting
Skip counting (pre-multiplication)
Communication and verbalization of findings
Problem solving
Reasoning and proof

WORKSHEET ON ROD CODE WORDS

Grades: 1, 2

Name: _____ Date: _____

Write the code for the rod that matches each train of white rods. Then, find the value of each word in terms of white rods. The first problem has been completed for you.

❶

4W	10W	6W
P	O	D

Total Value = ___20 W___

❷

10W	2W	9W

Total Value = _____

W	for	White
R	for	Red
G	for	Green
P	for	Purple
Y	for	Yellow
D	for	Dark Green
K	for	blacK
N	for	browN
E	for	bluE
O	for	Orange

❸

1W	10W	2W	6W

Total Value = _____

❹

3W	2W	10W	1W	8W

Total Value = _____

❺

5W	10W	5W	10W

Total Value = _____

❻

1W	10W	2W	2W	5W

Total Value = _____

© Learning Resources, Inc. Idea Book for Cuisenaire® Rods at the Primary Level

Grades: 1,2

WORKSHEET MASTER FOR ROD CODE WORDS

Name: Date:

Write the code for the rod that matches each train of white rods. Find the value of each word in terms of white rods.

❶

Total Value = _____

❷

Total Value = _____

W	for	White
R	for	Red
G	for	Green
P	for	Purple
Y	for	Yellow
D	for	Dark Green
K	for	blacK
N	for	browN
E	for	bluE
O	for	Orange

❸

Total Value = _____

❹

Total Value = _____

❺

Total Value = _____

❻

Total Value = _____

Grades: K,1,2

EXPLORING SYMMETRY

Materials:
Cuisenaire® Rods for each child
1-cm Graph Paper, page 15
Crayons matching the rods for each child
A mirror for each child (optional)

Settings:
One child working individually
A small group, children working individually
A whole class, children working individually

Learning Experience:
Explain to the children the meaning of a line of symmetry by having them make some symmetric designs. The portions of the design on both sides of a line of symmetry match.

Another way of saying that two shapes have the same size and shape is to say that they are congruent. In other words, the two portions of a design on both sides of a line of symmetry are congruent. This is shown at right.

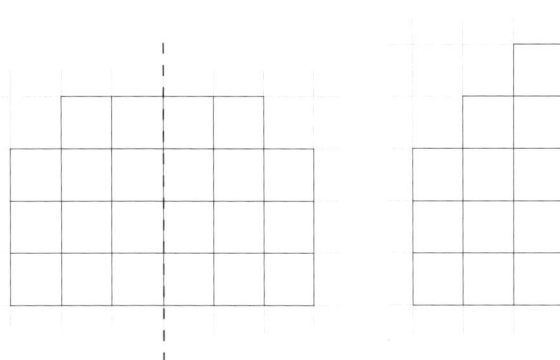

One Line of Symmetry

The dotted lines show the lines of symmetry for these designs. Some children will enjoy placing a mirror along the line of symmetry so as to view the other half of the design in the mirror.

In their free exploration with rods, children naturally create designs with lines of symmetry. Symmetry is so prevalent in nature, architecture, paintings, and interior decorating that children are exposed to many examples daily. Share a list on the bulletin board, with the name of the child who thought of each example.

Children should also be encouraged to create designs with two lines of symmetry. Encourage them to color symmetrical designs on 1-cm graph paper when ready.

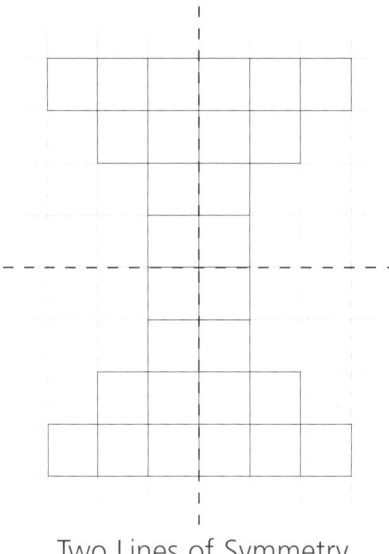

Two Lines of Symmetry

Underlying Mathematics Related to NCTM Standards:
Line of symmetry
Congruence of shapes
Connections to life
Visual thinking
Communication and verbalization of findings

Grades: K, 1, 2

MATCHING DESIGNS SIDE-BY-SIDE

Materials:
Cuisenaire® Rods for each child

Settings:
Two children working together
A small group, children working in pairs
A whole class, children working in pairs

Learning Experience:

Have each student pair sit side-by-side at a table or desk. A train of two orange rods should be placed between them to define a line of symmetry.

Ask one child to build a design with six rods on his or her side of the orange line. At least one of the six rods should touch the line. The other child matches the first child's design so that the two orange rods define a line of symmetry. Check to see that the children's completed design is symmetrical.

Then the children switch roles. The second child places six rods on his or her side of the line of symmetry. The first child completes the symmetrical design. Then, the children should exchange seats and repeat the activity. After doing this activity a few times, the children should be ready to play the Matching the Leader Game.

Rules for the Matching the Leader Game:
1. Partners sit side-by-side at a table or desk with a train of two orange rods placed between them to define a line of symmetry.
2. One child starts to build a design on one side of the line by placing one rod in position. The rod does not need to touch the orange rods, nor does it need to be placed horizontally or vertically. The second child must place a rod of the same color on the other side of the line of symmetry so that it is symmetrical with the first child's rod.
3. The child places another rod on either side of the line. The second child matches it. Play continues with a design of up to eight rods each. If the second player misplaces a piece at any time, the first player scores one point.
4. The players switch roles, so that the second player becomes the leader. If the first player misplaces a piece at any time, the second player scores a point.
5. The first player to score five points is the winner. After each round, the players should change the seating arrangement.

Underlying Mathematics Related to NCTM Standards:
Line of symmetry
Congruence of shapes
Connections to life
Visual thinking
Communication and verbalization of findings

COVERING DESIGNS IN MORE THAN ONE WAY

Grade: K, 1, 2

Materials:
Worksheet on Covering Designs in More Than One Way 1, page 102
Worksheet on Covering Designs in More Than One Way 2, page 103
1-cm Graph Paper for each child, page 15
Cuisenaire® Rods for each child
Pencil for each child
Crayons matching the rod colors for each child

Settings:
Two children working individually
A small group, children working individually
A whole class, children working individually

Learning Experience:

Addition work with more than two addends can be done in conjunction with geometric work. The Worksheets on pages 102 and 103 have the children cover each design with rods and then find the total value of all of the rods in each design in terms of white rods.

To find the total value, some children may wish to make a long train and match it with a train of orange rods plus another rod. Some may put the train along a number line or metric ruler. Many will be able to write the correct addition sentence immediately and do the adding in their heads. The addition can be done in several ways. This exercise builds readiness for multiplication as repeated addition, since more than one rod of the same color is often used within a single design.

Each design should be covered in several different ways, such as placing all rods horizontally, then vertically, and then mixed. For more designs, use the building and coloring experiences saved from previous activities. It is also fun for children to use the rods to make the capital letters of the alphabet or their own names or initials. Then, ask the children to make a design of something that begins with each letter of the alphabet, for example:

airplane	boat	crane	dragon	elephant	frog
garage	hat	igloo	jellyfish	kite	lion
monster	nine	owl	pumpkin	quilt	robot
submarine	truck	unicorn	vampire	whale	xylophone
yacht	zebra				

This activity can be extended to a challenge by asking the children to make a design for which the total value is a given number of white rods. Encourage them to color these designs on 1-cm graph paper and compare the differences. Different sets of rods will be chosen. If the same set of rods is used, the rods can be put in many different non-congruent configurations. This activity can also be extended to practicing money skills. This can be done by having the children find the value of a design if each white rod costs $1 and each red costs $2, etc.

Underlying Mathematics Related to NCTM Standards:
Filling space with rods
Problem solving
Representation of length in terms of white rods
Communication and verbalization of ideas
Sums with more than two addends
Money values
Multiplication as repeated addition
Connections between arithmetic and geometry

Grades: K, 1, 2

WORKSHEET ON COVERING DESIGNS IN MORE THAN ONE WAY 1

Name: Date:

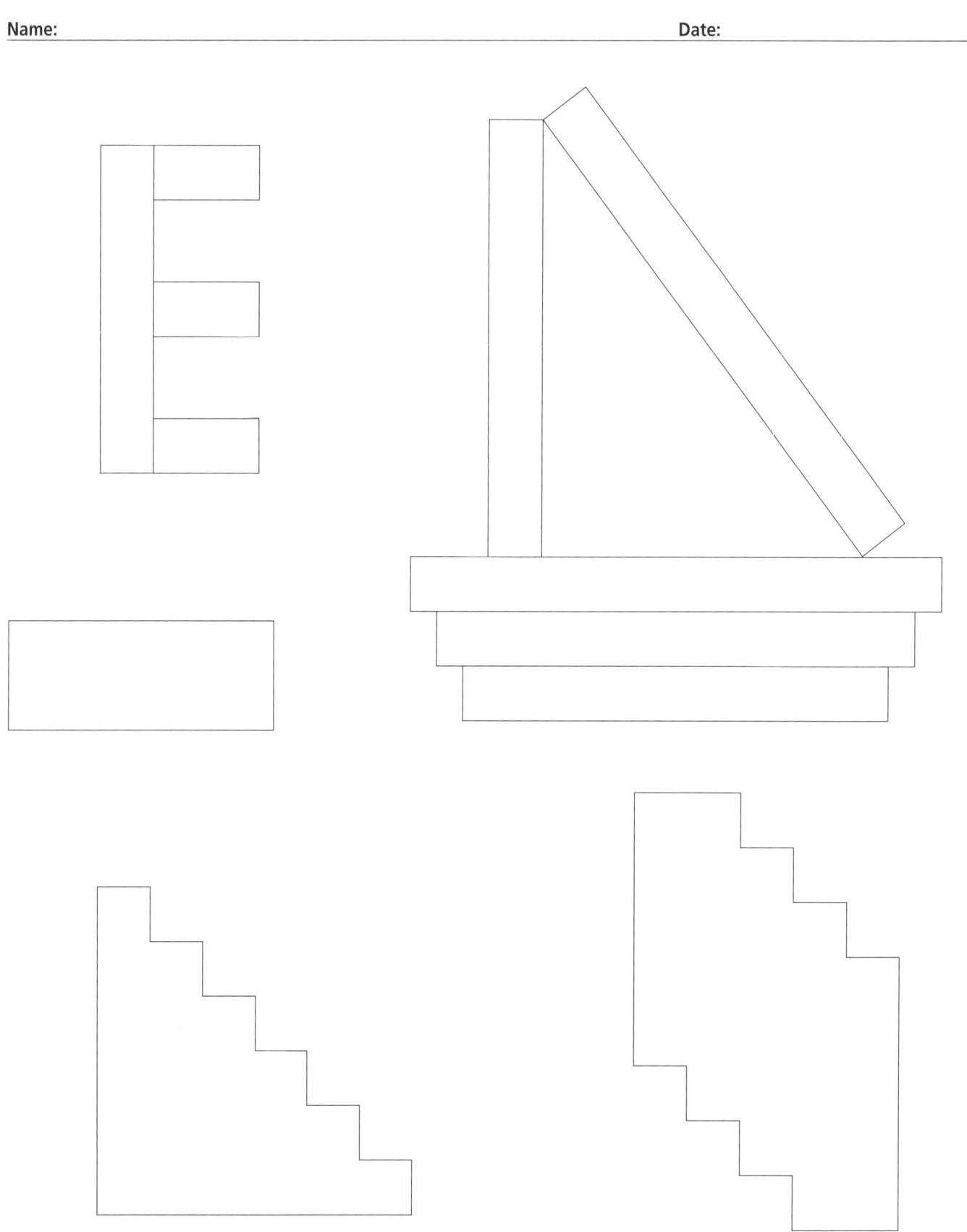

WORKSHEET ON COVERING DESIGNS IN MORE THAN ONE WAY 2

Name: _____ Date: _____

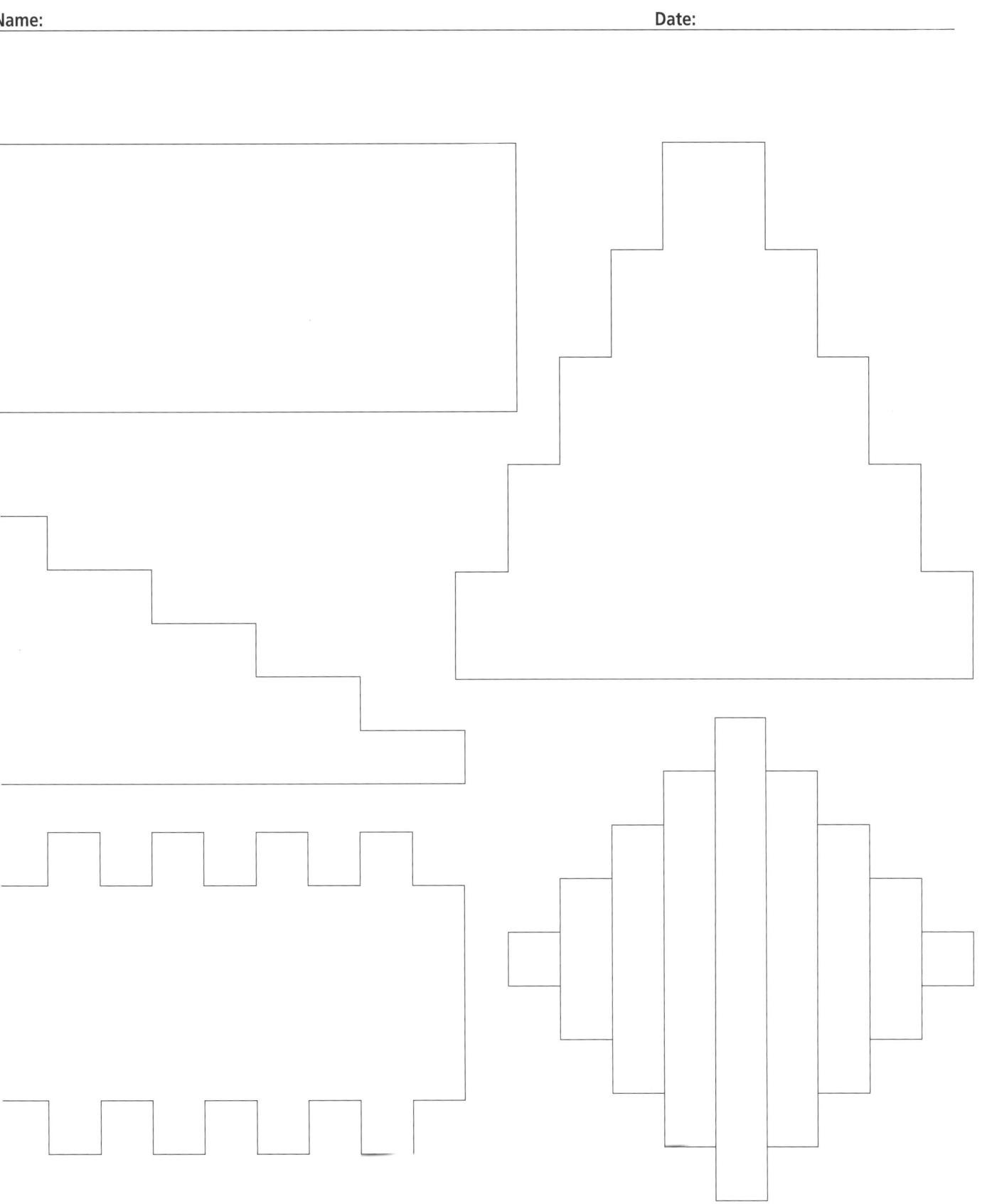

© Learning Resources, Inc. Idea Book for Cuisenaire® Rods at the Primary Level **103**

Grades: 1, 2

COVERING DESIGNS WITH A GIVEN SET OF RODS

Materials:

Worksheet on Covering Designs 1, page 105
Worksheet on Covering Designs 2, page 106
1-cm Graph Paper for each child, page 15
Cuisenaire® Rods for each child
Pencil for each child
Crayons matching the rod colors for each child

Settings:

Two children working individually
A small group, children working individually
A whole class, children working individually

Learning Experience:

The Worksheets on pages 105 and 106 specify the set of rods to be used to cover a particular design. Some designs can be done in more than one way, and some can be done in only one way. If the children are having difficulty, encourage them to place the longest rods first since they have the least flexibility.

Ask the children to color their designs or record the color codes on the design to show their solutions. Then have them compare their solutions to see which designs can be done in more than one way. Again, the children can compute the value of each design in terms of white rods.

Here is an example of a design that can be completed in more than one way (design 2. on page 105):

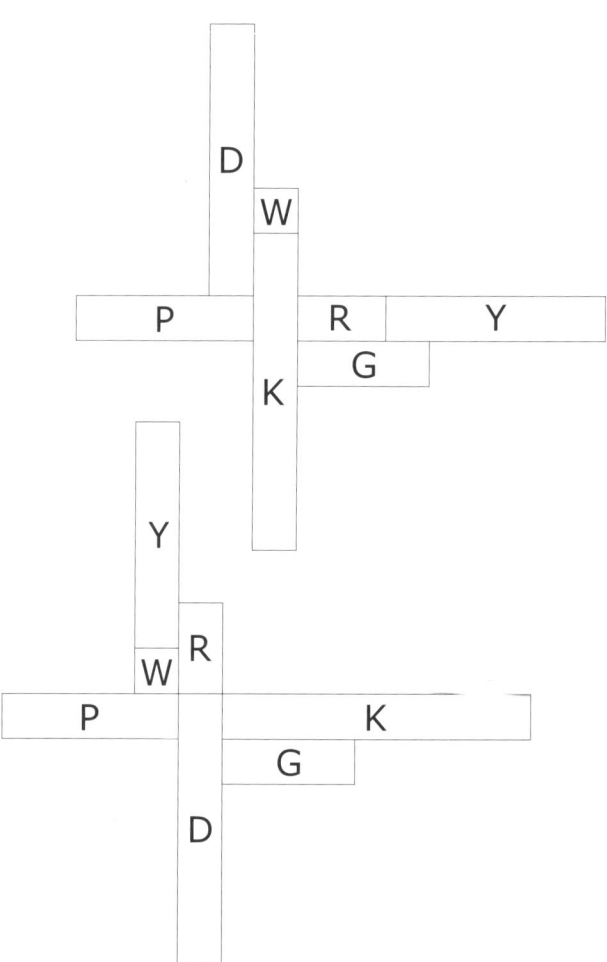

Children should be encouraged to make puzzles for their classmates on 1-cm graph paper by outlining the design with a black crayon and by listing the codes of the rods to be used.

Underlying Mathematics Related to NCTM Standards:

Filling space with rods
Representation of lengths in terms of white rods
Sums with more than two addends
Connections between arithmetic and geometry
Problem solving
Communication and verbalization of findings

WORKSHEET ON COVERING DESIGNS 1

Grades: 1, 2

Name: Date:

1. Use 1 W, 1 R, 1 G, 1 P, 1 Y

2. Use 1 W, 1 R, 1 G, 1 P, 1 Y, 1 D, 1 K

3. Use 2 G, 1 P, 1 Y, 1 D, 1 K, 1 N

4. Use 1 W, 1 R, 1 G, 1 P, 1 Y, 1 D, 1 K, 1 N

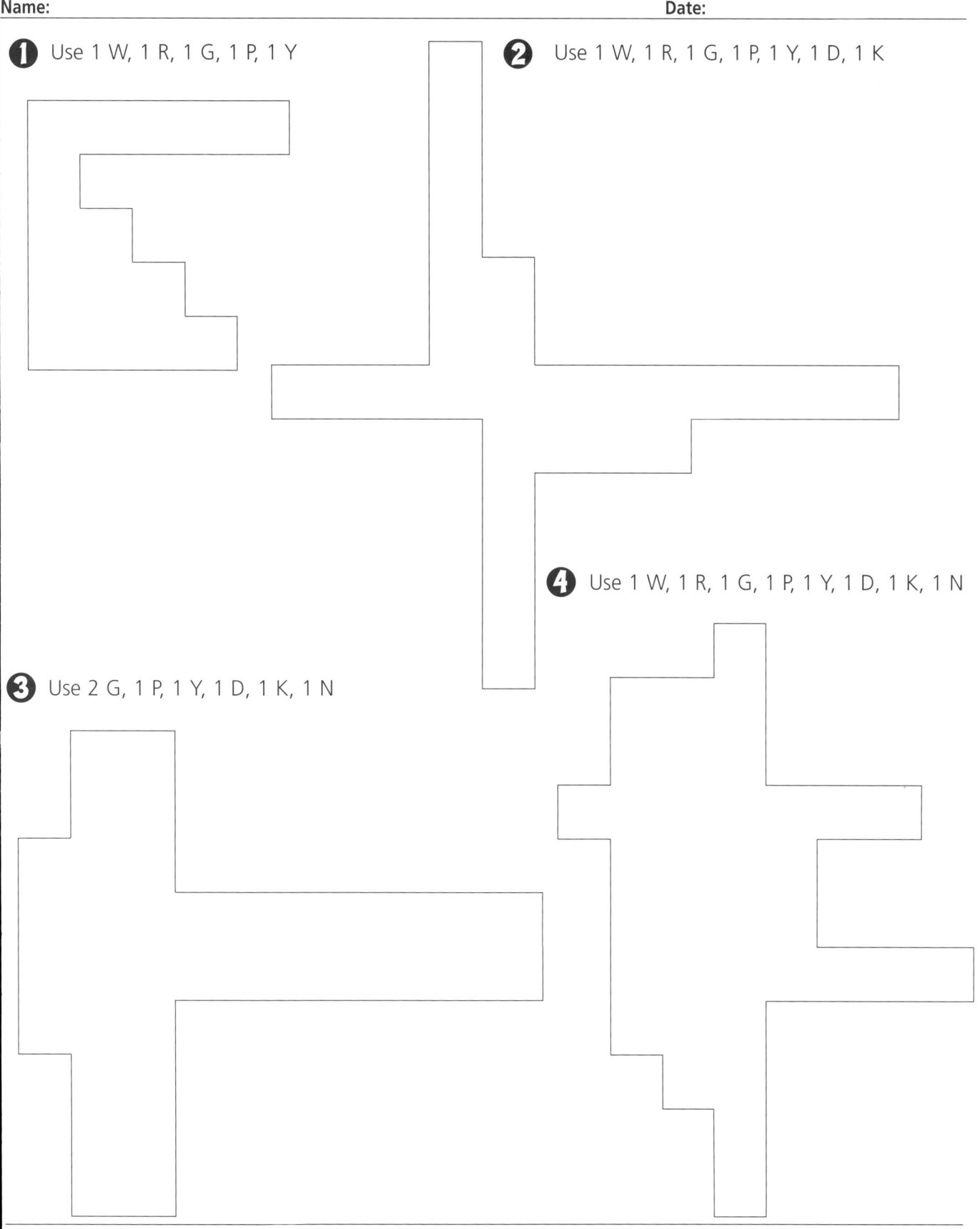

Grades: 1, 2

WORKSHEET ON COVERING DESIGNS 2

Name: Date:

❶ Use 1 W, 1 R, 1 G, 1 P, 1 Y, 1 D, 1 K, 1 E

❷ Use 1 W, 1 R, 1 G, 1 P, 1 Y, 1 D, 1 K, 1 N, 1 E, 1 O

❸ Use 1 R, 1 G, 1 P, 1 Y, 1 D, 1 K, 1 E

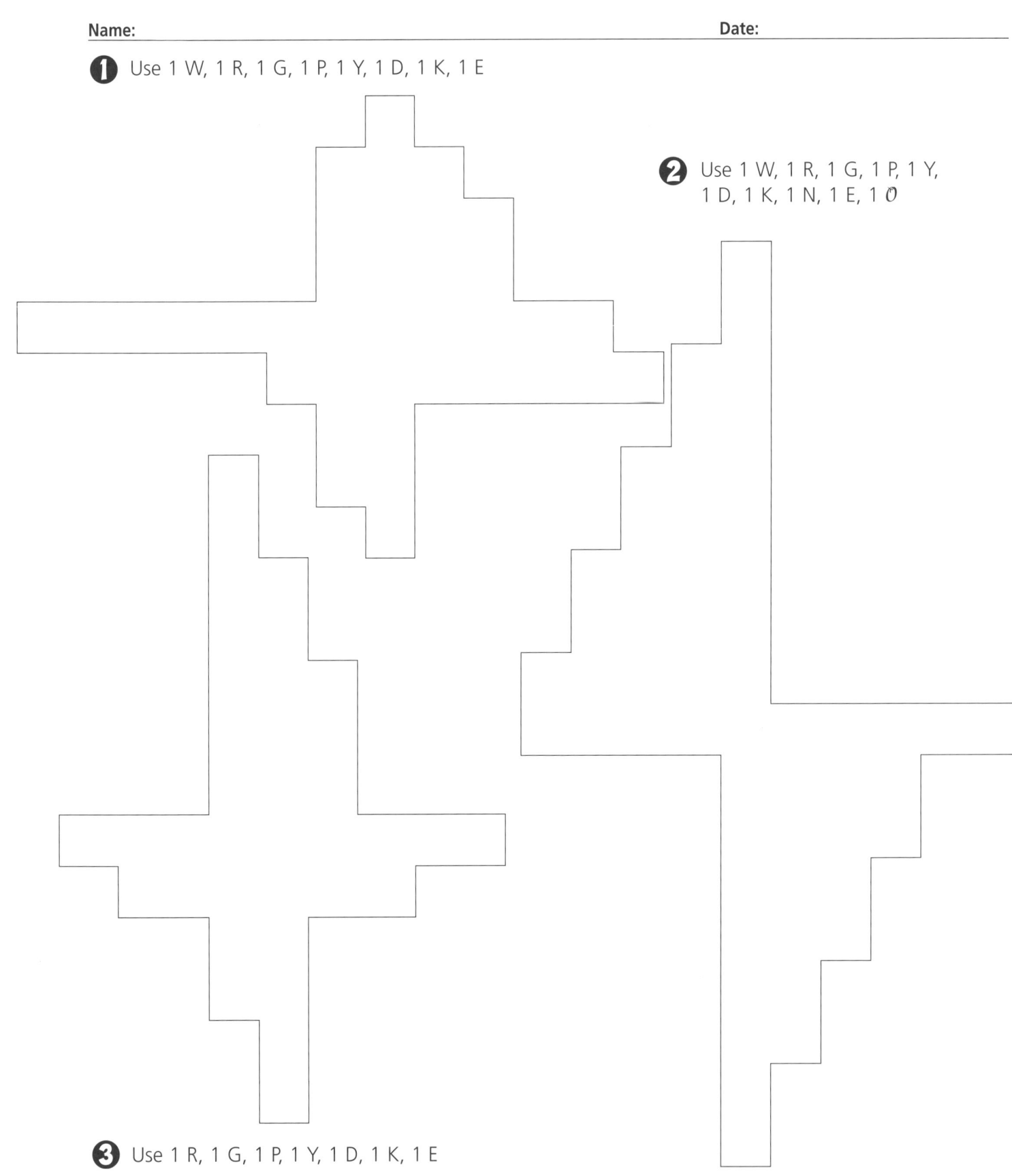

106 Idea Book for Cuisenaire® Rods at the Primary Level © Learning Resources, Inc.

COMPARING LENGTHS OF RODS

Grades: K, 1, 2

Materials:
Cuisenaire® Rods for each child
Cuisenaire® Rods for the teacher

Settings:
A small group led by the teacher
A whole class led by the teacher

Learning Experience:

Choose a yellow rod and a blue rod and place them side-by-side. Tell the children that the yellow rod is less than the blue rod since the yellow rod is shorter than the blue. Ask the children to find other rods less than the blue rod. (All possible answers include white, red, green, purple, yellow, dark green, black, and brown.)

Choose another rod and ask the children to find all the rods less than it. Children should be able to prove the inequality by placing the rods side-by-side. In finding all rods less than a given rod, some children will discover that it is possible to select an appropriate portion of a staircase. To promote classroom discussion, ask the following questions:

- Is there any rod that does not have a rod less than it? (Answer: white)
- Is there any rod less than all other rods? (Answer: white)
- All of these rods (random handful) are less than what rod?

Now compare a yellow rod and a blue rod the other way around by stating that the blue rod is greater than the yellow rod since the blue rod is longer than the yellow rod. Ask the children to find other rods greater than the yellow rod. (All possible answers include dark green, black, brown, and orange.) Hold up another rod and have the children respond by holding up any rod greater than it. Have the children prove each inequality by placing the rods side-by-side. Next, have them find all the rods between yellow and blue (dark green, black, and brown). Promote classroom discussion with the following questions:

- What two rods have the most rods between them? (Answer: white and orange)
- Name two rods for which there is no rod between them in length. (Answer: any consecutive rods in a staircase)

Children should be encouraged to ask each other questions so that they have the opportunity to use the vocabulary of <u>less than</u>, <u>greater than</u>, and <u>between</u>.

Underlying Mathematics Related to NCTM Standards:
Inequalities (less than, greater than, and between)
Comparison of lengths
Ordering of lengths
Problem solving
Reasoning and proof
Communication and verbalization of findings

Using Rods to Measure Objects

Grades: K, 1, 2

Materials:
Cuisenaire® Rods for each child
Pencil and paper for each child
Meter Stick (optional)

Settings:
A small group, led by the teacher
A whole class, led by the teacher

Learning Experience:

Children enjoy using one-color trains to measure the lengths of various objects. Start this Learning Experience by having each student pair measure the length of their desk using a one-color train of orange rods. Ask, "How many orange rods are almost enough? How many orange rods are just too much?"

Children may give their answers in terms of the number of orange rods. For example, "The desk is between 5 and 6 orange rods." The answer might also be given as an orange plus train. For example, the length may be close to 5 orange rods plus a black rod. If the children have a meter stick, they may see that this length is really close to 57 centimeters. (Note that each orange rod has a length of 10 centimeters. It is not appropriate to deal in centimeters for most of the children at these ages, but a few may be advanced to do so.)

Now measure this same length using a one-color train of yellow rods. Since it takes 2 yellow rods to match an orange rod, the children can anticipate that it will take about twice as many yellow rods. (For example, this time the length might be between 11 yellow rods and 12 yellow rods. Counting by 5s, the children can state that the length is between 55 whites and 60 whites, or 55 to 60 centimeters.) Such a long length requires too many white rods to lay end-to-end, so it is better to use a longer rod like orange or yellow and translate the length into white rods (or centimeters.)

Have children measure shorter objects, and encourage them to decide what rod or rods would be appropriate measuring sticks. No matter how fine the measurement tool, measurements are not exact, so the concepts of "between" and "close to" are very important.

There are many objects in the classroom that the children can measure such as the length of a pencil, the dimensions of various books, and the dimension of your desk. When the height of an object is being measured, children may need to make a mark to denote the end of each rod and the beginning of the next one.

Underlying Mathematics Related to NCTM Standards:
Equivalence of lengths
Close approximations of lengths
Counting by 10s and 5s
Reasoning and proof
Communication and verbalization of findings

PRACTICING INEQUALITY SIGNS

Grades: 1, 2

Learning Experience:

Choose two rods. Ask the children to place the two rods side-by-side and to describe the inequality relationship between the two rods.

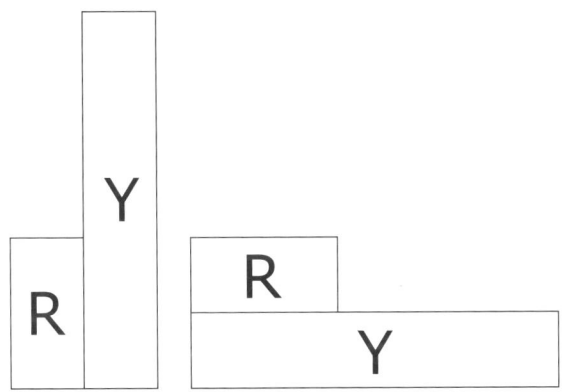

Red is <u>less than</u> yellow

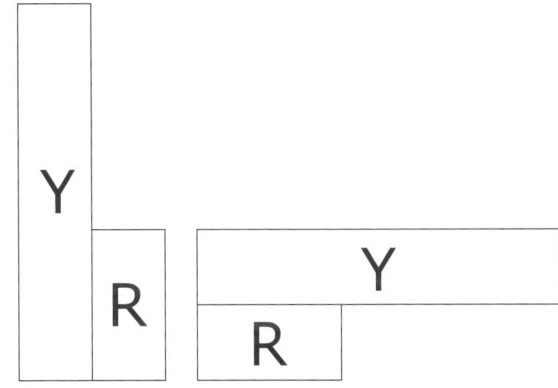

Yellow is <u>greater than</u> red

Explain that rods (and numbers) are often compared and a shorthand way of describing the relationship describes this:

< means is <u>less than</u>
> means is <u>greater than</u>

These symbols can be thought of as an extension of mathematical codes. Children should have the concepts of less than and greater than well established before learning to write the symbols. Eventually they will develop proficiency in reading R < Y as "red is less than yellow" and Y > R as "yellow is greater than red." When children are ready to use the symbols with numbers, they can give the value in terms of a white rod being considered as 1, stating that 2 < 5, read as "2 is less than 5" or 5 > 2, read as "5 is greater than 2."

If two rods of the same color are chosen, then the relationship is one of equality rather than inequality. For example: dark green = dark green, or in numbers 6 = 6. If two numbers are chosen randomly and are written down with a space between them, exactly one of the three relationships, <, >, or =, can be written between them to make a true sentence.

Give the children number sentences to complete using the <, >, or = sign. They can check their answers using the corresponding rod lengths.

Underlying Mathematics Related to NCTM Standards:
Inequalities (less than, greater than)
Comparison of lengths
Equality
Reasoning and proof
Use of inequality symbols
Communication and verbalization of findings

Grades: 1, 2

PLAYING THE COMPARING GAME

Materials:
Cuisenaire® Rods for each child
An empty container for each child

Settings:
Two children working together
A small group, children working in pairs
A whole class, children working in pairs

Learning Experience:

Ask the partners to share the rods so that each child has 2 rods of each color. Each child places the rods in an empty container and holds it under the table, out of sight. One child counts to three. On the count of three, each child takes one rod from the container and puts it on the table. The two rods are compared. The player with the longer rod wins both rods. The winner should state the inequality using both the color names and the number names. If the two rods are equal in length, they are discarded and no one wins rods on that turn.

The children take turns counting to three. If the timing isn't right on a turn and a rod is seen before the other rod is chosen, simply start the turn over. The game ends when all the rods in the containers have been used. Each partner makes a train by putting the rods won end-to-end. The player with the longer train wins the game. Children can add up their scores and tell how much the winner won by.

For variation, the player with the shorter rod wins both rods, and the player with the shorter train wins the game. It is important that children do not get the impression that more of something is always better. Children will like to alternate games and eventually alternate on each turn whether the win is the longer or shorter rod. The strategies are challenging and fun.

After children become proficient at the game, players may be asked to compare the two rods on a turn and tell how much longer one rod is than the other. This extension provides practice with the concepts of missing addends and subtraction developed on pages 64 through 81.

Underlying Mathematics Related to NCTM Standards:
One-to-one correspondence
Comparison of lengths
Inequalities (less than, greater than)
Equality
Addition and subtraction
Communication and verbalization of findings
Reasoning and proof

FINDING AREA OF A ROD DESIGN

Grades: 1, 2

Materials:
Worksheet on Area, page 112
1-cm Graph Paper, page 15
Cuisenaire® Rods for each child

Settings:
Two children working together
A small group, children working pairs
A whole class, children working in pairs

Learning Experience:

Ask each pair of children to take a yellow rod and to outline it on the 1-cm graph paper. Ask them to count the number of squares in this two-dimensional shape. There are five. This represents the area of the "footprint" of a yellow rod. The area is 5 square units.

In other words, a yellow rod covers 5 square units of area. Now ask the children to make various designs using two yellow rods and to trace around their designs on 1-cm graph paper. More than one design can be made. The area in each case is 10 square units.

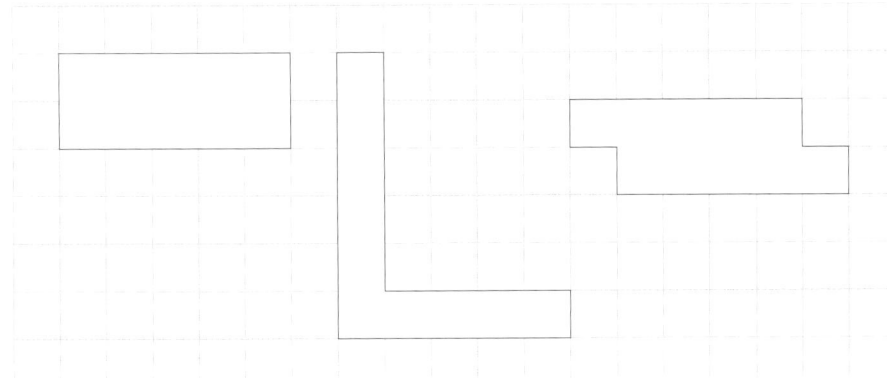

Answer Key

Worksheet on Area, page 112

1. 26 square units
2. 34 square units
3. 25 square units
4. 34 square units
5. 34 square units

Invite children to find the area of a rod design in more than one way by using different sets of rods to cover the design. The area can be counted in many different ways depending on the rods used.

For example: Using a purple, dark green, and black rod to cover the design at right, the children will find the area to be 4 + 6 + 7 square units or 17 square units. Placing rods vertically, they would use 4 green rods, 2 red rods and 1 white rod, equaling 12 + 4 + 1 square units or 17 square units. No matter what rods are used to cover the design, the total number of squares covered will be 17.

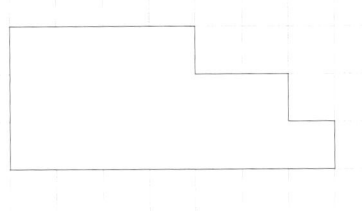

After completing the Worksheet on page 112, children can trace around their own designs to make area problems for their classmates. They should check their areas by covering the design with rods in more than one way.

Underlying Mathematics Related to NCTM Standards:
Concept of area
Problem solving
Counting
Adding with many addends
Communication and verbalization of findings
Reasoning and proof

Grades: 1, 2

WORKSHEET ON AREA

Name: Date:

Cover up the designs below with your rods. Then find the area by adding the rod numbers together.

❶

Area = _____ Square Units

❷

Area = _____ Square Units

❸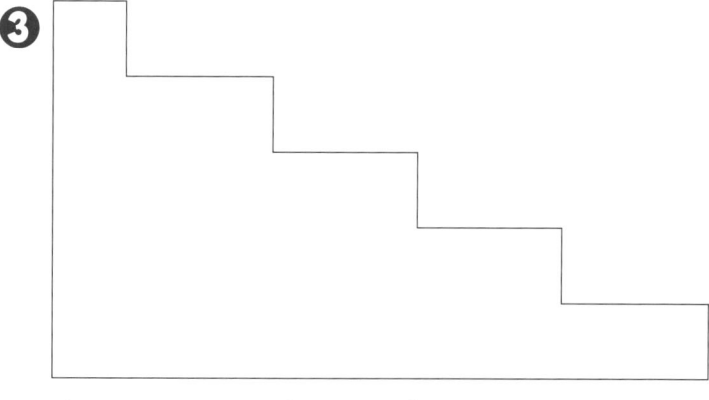

Area = _____ Square Units

❹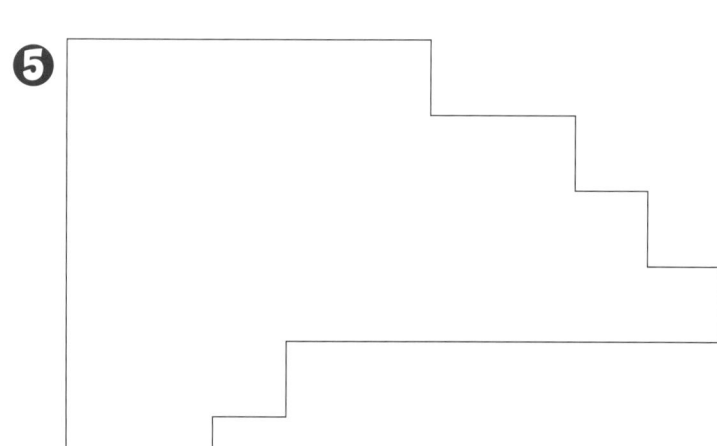

Area = _____ Square Units

❺

Area = _____ Square Units

Grades: 1, 2

FINDING PERIMETER OF A ROD DESIGN

Materials:
Cuisenaire® Rods for each child
Worksheet on Perimeter, page 114
1-cm Graph Paper for each child, page 15

Settings:
Two children working together
A small group, children working in pairs
A whole class, children working in pairs

Learning Experience:

Ask each pair of children to take a yellow rod and to outline it on the 1-cm graph paper. Ask them to count the number of units there are in the outline of a yellow rod.
There are 12. This represents the perimeter of the outline of a yellow rod.

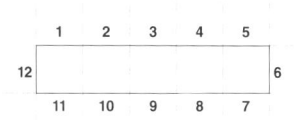

Now ask the children to make a design using two yellow rods and to trace around the design on 1-cm graph paper. Ask the children, "What is the perimeter of your design?"

In contrast to the area of any design made with two yellow rods always being 10 square units, the perimeters are not always the same. The examples at right show the difference in perimeter.

All the designs on the Worksheet on page 114 were made with the same three rod colors: green, purple, and yellow. All of these designs have the same area (3 + 4 + 5 square units or 12 square units), but no two designs are congruent to each other. The designs may or may not have different perimeters. Have the children count the number of units of length in the outline of each design and discuss their findings.

Challenge students to make another design with the same rods but having a different perimeter, such as 20 or 24 units. They should notice that the more compact the design, the smaller the perimeter.

Note: When using Connecting Cuisenaire® Rods to find perimeter, do not count the connectors.

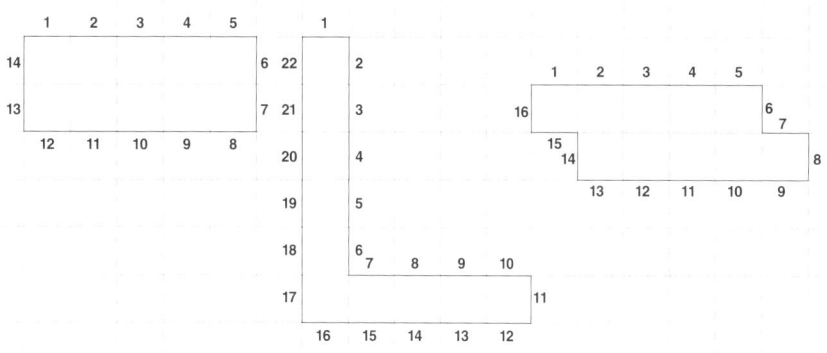

Underlying Mathematics Related to NCTM Standards:
Concept of perimeter
Relationship between area and perimeter
Counting
Reasoning and proof
Communication and verbalization of findings

Answer Key
Worksheet on Perimeter, page 114

1. 18 units
2. 16 units
2. 22 units
4. 18 units

Grades: 1, 2

WORKSHEET ON PERIMETER

Name: _____   Date: _____

These rod designs can be made with the same three rod colors: green, purple, and yellow. Find the perimeter of each rod design. The designs are on centimeter graph paper to help you count the total length around.

 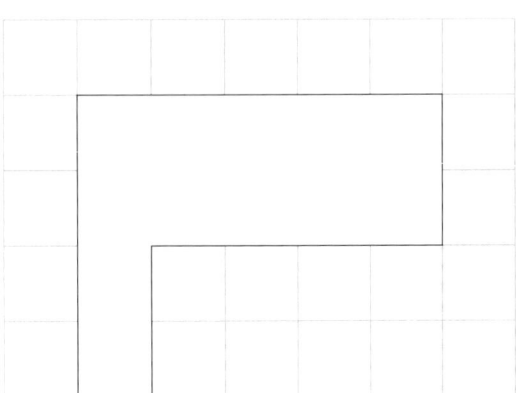

Perimeter = _____ Units

 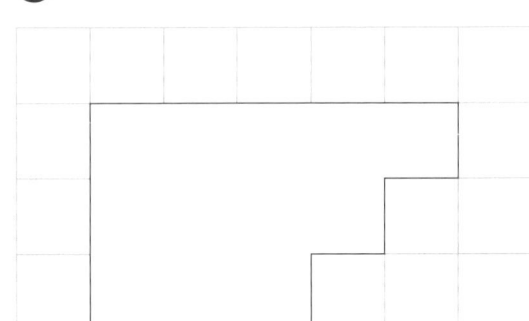

Perimeter = _____ Units

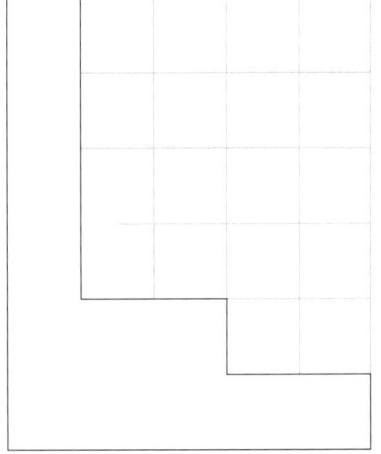 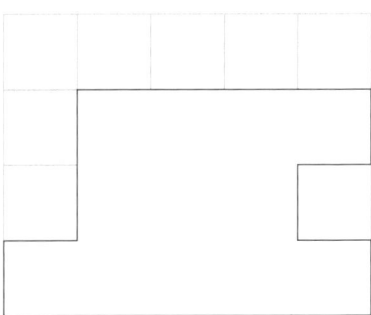

Perimeter = _____ Units

Perimeter = _____ Units

Place a green, purple, and yellow rod on each design to verify that the area of each design is 12 square units.

CONDUCTING SURVEYS

Grades: K, 1, 2

Materials:
Cuisenaire® Rods for each child
Extra white rods for each group
Blank paper and pencil for each group

Settings:
A small group led by the teacher
A whole class led by the teacher

Learning Experience:

Children enjoy conducting surveys among their classmates or among all the students in the school in their grade. To prepare for doing surveys, they need to ask a question, establish the possible categories for the responses, and know how to tally the responses. It may even involve refining the question and the categories by taking a small sampling with another population.

For example, if the children want to know the kinds of pets that their classmates have, they might start with the categories of dogs, cats, gerbils, or birds. Then they may find that one of the households has 6 cats. Is this counted as 1 or 6? If the question were "What kind of pets do my classmates have?" it would be counted as 1 for cats. If the question is "How many pets do my classmates have and what kinds?" the answer would be counted as 6 for cats.

Also, it may turn out that someone has a guinea pig or snake. If they live on a farm, they might have a pet lamb or a pet goat. The categories could be expanded or a category labeled as "Other" could be used.

Once the question is well-defined and once the categories are set up, children should label a sheet of unlined paper for each category and then place one white rod on the appropriate paper for each response. Some children may also wish to learn how to make tally marks by fives for the data.

Other surveys can be done around favorite TV shows, favorite ice cream flavors, months of birthdays, etc. Children will enjoy doing surveys throughout the entire school year and then telling or writing stories about their findings.

Animal	Number of Classmates Who Own One	Total Number of Classmates
Dogs	﹉﹉ ll	7
Cats	﹉﹉ ﹉﹉ ll	12
Gerbils	lll	3
Birds	ll	2
Other	﹉﹉	5

Underlying Mathematics Related to NCTM Standards:
Categorization
Counting
One-to-one correspondence
Problem solving
Connections to life situations
Communication and verbalization of findings

Grades: K, 1, 2

USING RODS FOR BAR GRAPHS

Materials:
Cuisenaire® Rods for each group
Crayons matching the rod colors for each group
1-cm Graph Paper, page 15

Settings:
A small group led by the teacher
A whole class led by the teacher

Learning Experience:
The rods lend themselves naturally to making bar graphs. After the children have learned how to conduct surveys and how to organize the data using a white Cuisenaire Rod per response as described on page 115, they can now replace the white rods with an equivalent one-car train (or orange-plus train) in preparation for making a bar graph. Give the children a choice of:

1. Placing the categories on the vertical axis and making horizontal bars with the rods, or
2. Placing the categories on the horizontal axis and making vertical bars with the rods.

They should place the correct rods on the 1-cm graph paper in either bar graph and then color the rods on the graph paper. Bar graphs should be made for other data collected such as favorite TV shows, favorite ice cream flavors, months of birthdays, etc.

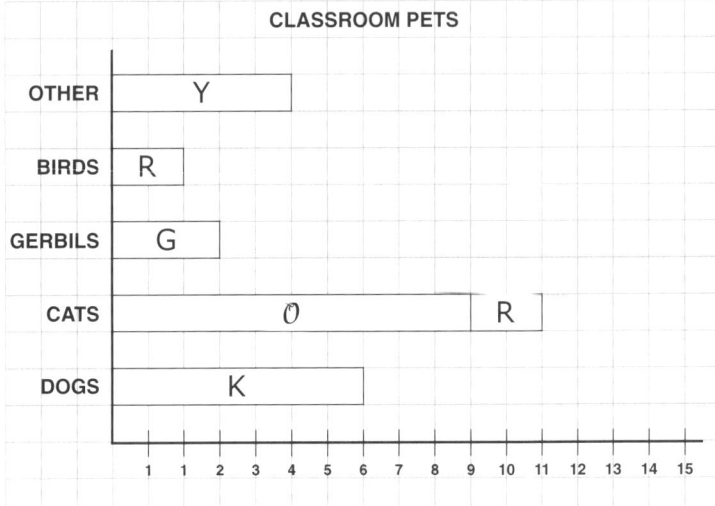

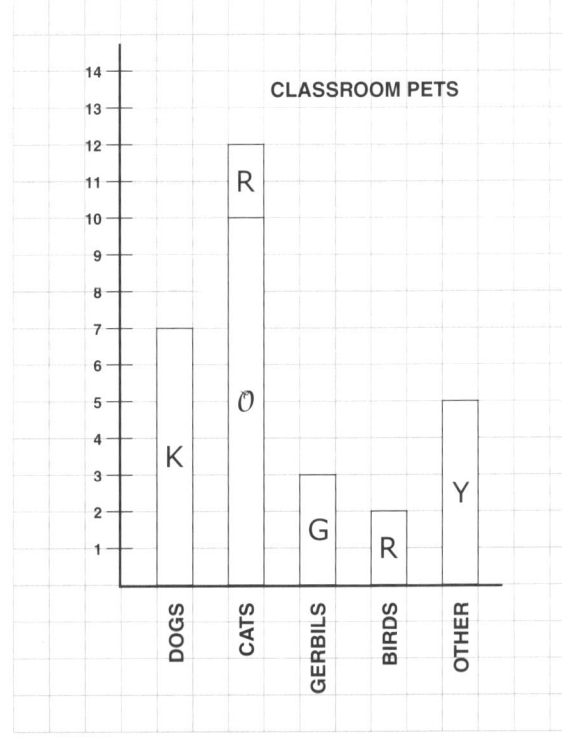

Underlying Mathematics Related to NCTM Standards:
Categorization
One-to-one correspondence
Equivalence of lengths
Counting
Problem solving
Connections to life situations
Communication and verbalization of findings

Grades: 1, 2

FINDING REARRANGEMENTS OF RODS IN A TRAIN

Materials:
Cuisenaire® Rods for each group
Crayons matching the rod colors for each group
1-cm Graph Paper for each group, page 15

Settings:
A small group led by the teacher
A whole class led by the teacher

Learning Experience:

Ask the children to choose a red rod, a white rod, and a yellow rod, and to make a train with these three rods. Then ask the children to build all the possible trains using these three colors and to describe them orally by naming the rods.

Remind the students to name a train by naming each rod from left to right. For example:

red, white, yellow   white, red, yellow   yellow, white, red
red, yellow, white   white, yellow, red   yellow, red, white

Now try three other colors, such as green, red, and purple, and have the children build and name the six different arrangements of colors.

Let the children choose three other colors. Ask, "Are there still six different trains?" (The answer is yes.) They may want to confirm that for two rods, there are just two possible arrangements. Some children may want to try four colors such as red, green, purple, and yellow to see how many of the 24 possible trains they can make and color on centimeter graph paper. The design that the rods make is pretty, especially if the rearrangements are done systematically.

One of the topics taught in probability is permutations, the making of rearrangements of a set of objects. The number of possible arrangements is written as a factorial and the notation is an exclamation point, !. The notation 3! is read "three factorial." For three objects, the number of possible arrangements is $3! = 3 \times 2 \times 1 = 6$. This is displayed in the following example: If three containers each hold one rod, there are three choices for the first container. Once chosen, there are two choices left for the second container, and only one choice left for the last container. For four objects, the number of possible arrangements is $4! = 4 \times 3 \times 2 \times 1 = 24$. If there are five objects, the number of possible arrangements is $5! = 5 \times 4 \times 3 \times 2 \times 1 = 120$.

It is important for teachers to know the factorial notation and its meaning since children who have calculators wonder what the exclamation point means and when it gets used.

Underlying Mathematics Related to NCTM Standards:
Permutations (arrangements of rod patterns)
Visual thinking
Patterns
Problem solving
Reasoning and proof
Communication and verbalization of findings

Grades: 1, 2

FINDING ALL THE TRAINS FOR A GIVEN ROD

Materials:
1-cm Graph Paper for each group, page 15
Cuisenaire® Rods for each group
Crayons matching the rod colors for each group

Settings:
A small group, children working individually
A whole class, children working individually

Learning Experience:

Ask the children to take a purple rod and to make all the possible matching trains. Sort and count the trains according to whether they are one-car trains, two-car trains, three-car trains, or four-car trains. For example, there are 8 possible trains for purple, sorted into the following piles according to the number of cars.

Train Equivalencies to the Purple Rod
  1 one-car train: purple
  3 two-car trains: red+red, white+green, green+white
  3 three-car trains: red+white+white, white+white+red, white+red+white
  1 four-car train: white+white+white+white

Now have the children find and color the possible trains for a yellow rod as shown above. There are 16 possible trains for a yellow rod (1 one-car train, 4 two-car trains, 6 three-car trains, 4 four-car trains, and 1 five-car train).

An important application of Pascal's Triangle is the number of subsets in a set (known as the study of combinations in probability). Suppose you have a set with three rods, red, white, and green. There is 1 subset that contains none of these three rods. There are 3 possible subsets that contain just one of the rods. There are 3 possible subsets that contain two of the rods at a time (white and red, white and green, red and green), and 1 possible subset (the original set itself) that contains all three rods.

These patterns should be colored and saved for further exploration related to Pascal's Triangle as described on page 119. The numbers in Pascal's Triangle have fascinating patterns and appear in many mathematical contexts. It is helpful for children to learn about Pascal's Triangle early and in a concrete context like patterns with rods.

Another important application of Pascal's Triangle is the number of subsets in a set (known as the study of combinations in probability). Suppose you have a set with the three rods: white, red and green. There is **1** subset that contains none of these three rods. There are **3** possible subsets that contain just one of the rods. There are **3** possible subsets that contain two of the rods at a time (white and red, white and green, red and green), and **1** possible subset (the original set itself) that contains all three rods.

Underlying Mathematics Related to NCTM Standards:
Association of various addends for a sum
Permutations (arrangements of rod patterns)
Patterns
Problem solving
Communication and verbalization of findings
Combinations (forming subsets of a given set)

EXPLORING PASCAL'S TRIANGLE

Grade: 2

Materials:
Centimeter Graph Paper, page 15
Cuisenaire® Rods for each group
Crayons matching the rod colors per group

Settings:
A small group led by the teacher
A whole class led by the teacher

Learning Experience:

The patterns for the number of possible trains for a given rod are predictable according to the numbers in Pascal's Triangle.

The white rod has just **1** one-car train.
The red rod has **1** one-car train and **1** two-car train.
The green rod has **1** one-car train, **2** two-car trains, and **1** three-car train.
The purple rod has **1** one-car train, **3** two-car trains, **3** three-car trains, and **1** four-car train.
The yellow rod has **1** one-car train, **4** two-car trains, **6** three-car trains, **4** four-car trains, and **1** five-car train.

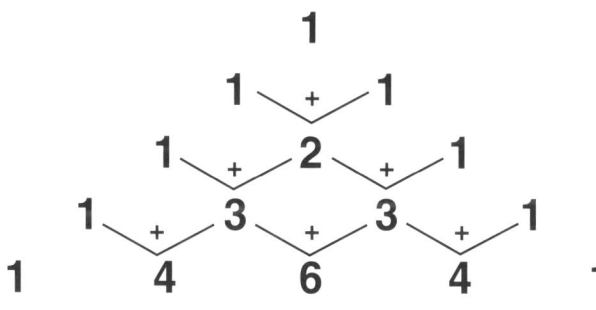

The pattern can be continued to predict the arrangements for the dark green rod. The next row of Pascal's Triangle (found by placing 1s at both ends and obtaining the inner numbers by adding the two numbers just above) is 1, 5, 10, 10, 5, 1. The groups of children can split up the work to make and color all these patterns with rods. Some children will enjoy the number patterns and others will enjoy the artistic aspects of this activity since the colored designs look like colorful rugs.

The total number of possible trains for a given rod can be found by adding the numbers in the appropriate row of Pascal's Triangle. The results are white (1), red (2), green (4), purple (8), yellow (16), and dark green (32). These are special numbers called the powers of two. For example, 8 = 2 x 2 x 2 or 2 to the third power.

Underlying Mathematics Related to NCTM Standards:
Association of various addends for a sum
Powers of two
Permutations (arrangements of rod patterns)
Problem solving
Communication and verbalization of findings

Grades: 1, 2

EXPLORING PROBABILITY WITH ROD CODES

Materials:
Class list of first names
Index cards for each group
Blank paper and pencil for each group

Settings:
A small group led by the teacher
A whole class led by the teacher

Learning Experience:

Review the rod codes with the children: **W R G P Y D K N E O**. Then ask the children to think of first names made entirely with the rod letters like KEN, DON, GWEN, KENNY, OWEN, NED, RON, RONNY, ROGER, and PEGGY. Choose one of the names, such as GWEN, and write each letter on a separate index card. Then shuffle the cards and draw one randomly, replace it, and draw again and again. Each time you will get a rod code letter, so the probability of getting a rod code letter is 1.

Now take some examples of names that don't contain code letters, such as SAUL. Write each letter on a separate index card. Then shuffle the cards, draw one randomly, replace it, and draw again and again. You will never get a rod code letter, so this is a case where the probability is 0. Children should be taught that probability values always range from 0 to 1, inclusive. Now, have the children write the name of each child in the group and underline the rod code letters to compute the theoretical probability for the chances of getting a rod code letter.

Have children conduct random drawings to check how close the actual sampling results are to the theoretical probability. Each time a letter is drawn, it is recorded, and the letter is put back in the deck. The deck is then shuffled. Children should do a sample of about 100 draws per name. They will find that there is always a slight difference between the theoretical probability and the results of random sampling. Children love figuring out the chances of something occurring or not occurring. This activity can be done for many names.

The probabilities of getting any particular letter can also be computed and checked. For example, in the name C O N N I E, a rod code letter theoretically would be drawn 4 out of 6 times, the letter C would be 1 out of 6 times, the letter O would be 1 out of 6 times, the letter I would be 1 out of 6 times, the letter E would be 1 out 6 times, and the letter N would be 2 out of 6 times since there are two Ns in the name.

J A N E	2 chances out of 4	Probability = 2/4
A N N	2 chances out of 3	Probability = 2/3
P A U L	1 chance out of 4	Probability = 1/4
K A R E N	4 chances out of 5	Probability = 4/5
S H A W N	2 chances out of 5	Probability = 2/5
M A R I O N	3 chances out of 6	Probability = 3/6

Underlying Mathematics Related to NCTM Standards:
Rod code names
Problem solving
Expected outcomes
Reasoning and proof
Probability values between 0 and 1
Communication and verbalization of findings

Idea Book for Cuisenaire® Rods at the Primary Level